Mahan Air
Iran's Largest Airline

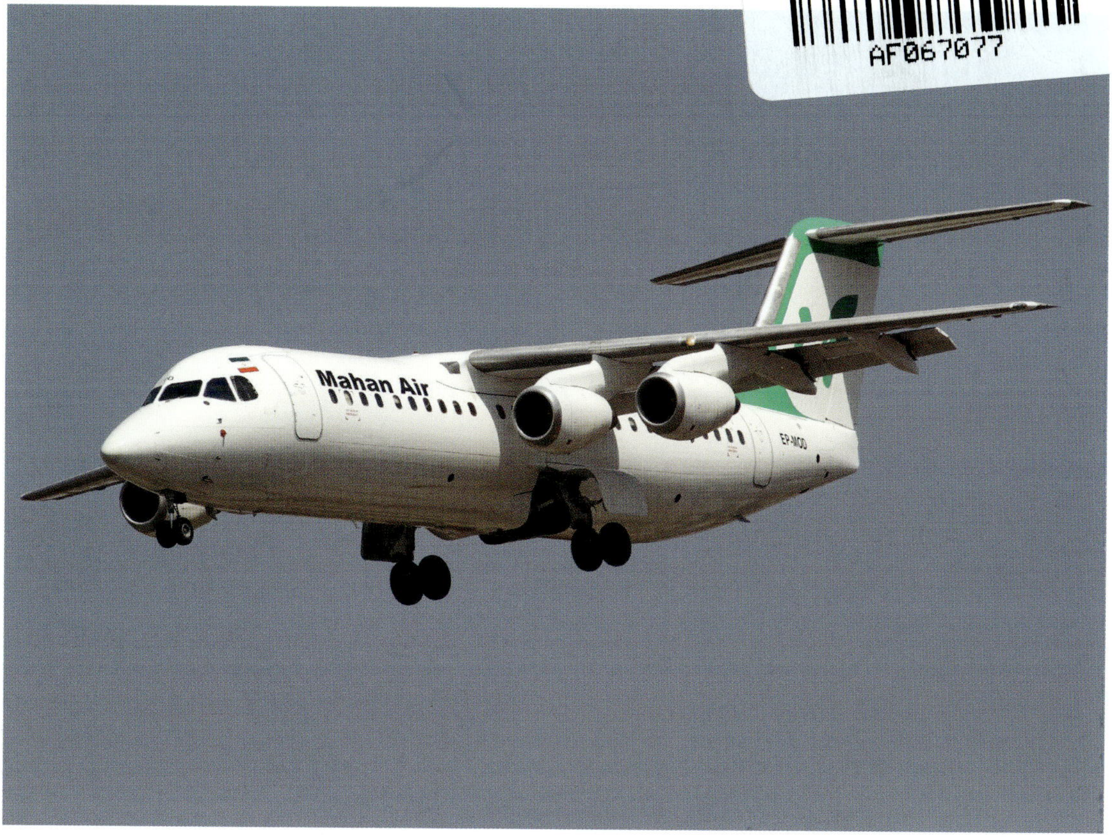

BABAK TAGHVAEE

KEY Books

AIRLINES SERIES, VOLUME 13

Front cover image: EP-MND was one of two Boeing 747-3B3M heavy passenger cargo aircraft transferred to ConViasa's Emtrasur Cargo in January 2022 and seized in Argentina at the request of the US government in June 2022. (Babak Taghvaee)

Title page image: EP-MOD is one of Mahan Air's BAe 146-300s, which has been in storage since 2014. (Babak Taghvaee)

Contents page image: EP-MNB is one of Mahan Air's three Boeing 747-422s. It has been in storage since 2021 and is seen here at Mehrabad airport on 21 July 2021. (Mahan Air)

Back cover image: EP-MNA is one of three Boeing 747-422 wide-body passenger aircraft. It is now active with the EP-MEE registration code. (Babak Taghvaee)

Published by Key Books
An imprint of Key Publishing Ltd
PO Box 100
Stamford
Lincs PE9 1XQ

www.keypublishing.com

The right of Babak Taghvaee to be identified as the author of this book has been asserted in accordance with the Copyright, Designs and Patents Act 1988 Sections 77 and 78.

Copyright © Babak Taghvaee, 2023

ISBN 978 1 80282 583 1

All rights reserved. Reproduction in whole or in part in any form whatsoever or by any means is strictly prohibited without the prior permission of the Publisher.

Typeset by SJmagic DESIGN SERVICES, India.

Contents

Introduction 4
Chapter 1 Early Years 5
Chapter 2 The Long-Haul Fleet Today 25
Chapter 3 Mahan's Single-Aisle Airliners 74
Appendix 1 Incidents and Accidents 92
Appendix 2 Mahan Air Fleet Details 94

Introduction

In December 2022, Mahan Air, with a fleet of 70 aircraft was the largest Iranian airline. Ten regional jets and three wide-body aircraft serve 26 domestic destinations. These, together with an additional 12 long-haul passenger aircraft, fly to 21 destinations internationally. Two Airbus A340-642 wide-body passenger aircraft and two Boeing 747-281F heavy cargo aircraft are in service with Venezuela's national airline ConViasa and Mahan Air-owned Iranian cargo line Fars Air Qeshm to provide passenger and cargo services particularly in Latin America, enabling the airline to have revenue from these markets.

Mahan Air is currently the most successful airline in Iran and has, in a relatively short time frame, expanded and developed its fleet to a level where it is able to fill the gap created by the fading presence of Iran Air in both domestic and international markets. The airline has received the special attention of the Islamic Republic of Iran and also Islamic Revolutionary Guard Corps (IRGC), which uses the airline's passenger aircraft. Disguised as passenger flights, the Quds Force branch of IRGC has used Mahan Air to transport troops and their weapons to Syria and Lebanon within the past several years resulting in the imposition of the toughest sanctions by the US government on the airline.

Despite the sanctions, Mahan Air currently has 33 out of its 70 aircraft operational. Among them, ten are jointly operated by ConViasa, Iran Air Tours and Syrian Airlines enabling both IRGC and Mola-al-Movahedin Charity Institute (the owner of Mahan Air) to profit from transporting cargo and passengers to and from Iran, Syria and Venezuela. With the direct support of the Iranian government, the airline supports the flag carriers of Syria and Venezuela to maintain, overhaul and operate some of their aircraft, which are missing spare parts or require heavy maintenance including C and D-checks (heavy maintenance) to be carried out on them.

Despite being a major source of income for its owners and shareholders including IRGC, the airline is a strategic asset of the Iranian government, supporting its regional and ultra-regional allies and expanding its hegemony in the Middle East and Latin America. The airline plays an important role in airlifting personnel, foreign proxies and weapons for the IRGC Quds Force. Mahan Air has associations with the covert operations of IRGC Quds Force, mimicking the work of Air America and Aeroflot on behalf of the CIA and KGB respectively, during the Cold War.

Despite being severely sanctioned, Mahan Air has expanded its fleet, procuring second-hand aircraft through a network of 'front' companies in various countries such as Armenia, Iraq, Kazakhstan, Kyrgyzstan, Ukraine and Uzbekistan within the past three decades. In this book, the history and current fate of the aircraft operated by Mahan Air and their service in supporting the operations of IRGC Quds Force is explained in detail.

Chapter 1
Early Years

Mahan Air's origins

Mahan Air was officially launched on 3 December 1994, one year after it received delivery of its first aircraft. It was created by Hossein Marashi, governor of Iran's Kerman province, and cousin of Effat Marashi, the wife of Ayatollah Akbar Hashemi Rafsanjani, who was then president of Iran's Islamic regime. The airline's first aircraft were a pair of Russian-made Tupolev Tu-154M passenger aircraft and an Il-76TD heavy cargo aircraft, obtained with the help of Egyptian company Cairo Charter and Cargo (later Cargo Aviation). The Egyptian company was a 50 percent shareholder of Mahan Air and provided aircraft in exchange for the paying down of Egyptian government debt, dating back prior to 1979, when Iran's Pahlavi government had given loans to Egypt.

About the selection of 'Mahan' as the name of the airline, Hossein Marashi recalled:

We thought about the name of the airline for about four months we wanted to find a name that would be suitable for the airline and show its authenticity from Kermani. Different names were suggested, including Bahr Aseman, which is the name of one of the heights of Kerman. One day, Mr. Mohajerani (Ata'ollah Mohajerani, former Minister of Culture and Islamic Guidance of the Islamic regime) came to Kerman and we asked him to suggest a name and he immediately told us to call it Mahan.

Donyaye Eqtesad newspaper,
17 November 2006

Mahan Air was formed and registered as a part of Mola al-Movahedin Charity (MMC), which had been created by the Marashi family and other figures close to Iran's Islamic government. Registering Mahan Air as an asset of a charitable organisation helped to make it tax exempt. The Quds Force branch of the IRGC became a major shareholder of MMC's companies including Mahan Air. This later enabled the military organisation to utilise assets of the airline for its operations overseas.

In April 2010, Hossein Marashi published his memory about the formation of Mahan Air:

When I was the governor of Kerman, I noticed the lack of air facilities (in our province). One day I was sitting in my office, when a friend called me from Dubai and said that an Egyptian man named Ebrahim Kamel has four planes and wants to establish an airline company in Iran and asked if you are ready to do this in Kerman. I agreed without hesitation. I immediately gave the necessary order to the head of Kerman airport, and the next day we sat down in the airport lounge and negotiated with the Egyptian side and agreed to form a joint venture on a 50-50 basis, on the condition that he would finance Iran's share and that we would be a creditor to take it from the company's income. The negotiation did not last more than a quarter of an hour and we finally reached an agreement.

Later we learned that the Iranian government had given several loans to the Egyptian government during the Shah's time, and that the Egyptian government could not repay the loans to Iran. Mr. Kamel told us that if we can get Iran's approval, he will also get Egypt's approval to buy these planes and give them to Iran. I immediately contacted Dr. Nawab in the Ministry of

Economy and he confirmed Iran's demand from Egypt. Dr. Nawab agreed to take delivery of the planes from Mr. Kamel instead of the debts. They went and got the approval of the Egyptian government. We also reported here to Mr. Nourbakhsh (Head of the Iranian National Bank) and I also informed Mr. Hashemi. Finally, by using this possibility, the Mola-al-Mohadin charity organization paid Iranian riyals to the government...

Author interview, Vatan Emrooz newspaper,
24 May 2014

In April 2010, Hossein Marashi claimed that MMC had paid US$149 million to the Iranian National Bank, effectively the value of the three aircraft that Egypt had given to the airline, but this was later revealed to be untrue. Tahmasb Mazaheri, former Minister of Economy of the government revealed on 16 March 2014 that MMC never paid the US$149 million to the Iranian government. Mazaheri shared his memory of how Hossein Marashi got approval of the government board to receive US$149 million of Egypt's debts in the form of three aircraft:

One day, during the meeting of the government board, they sent me a message asking me to come out for a few minutes to talk about something. I asked who the person was and they said Mr. Marashi, who was a Member of Parliament at that time. The discussion of the government meeting was so important that day that I should not leave the meeting. I sent a message that I can't leave the meeting now. We will see each other after the meeting (noon). After that, I saw that they brought a sheet of paper from outside the meeting in which they had collected the signatures of a number of members of the government on it as an approval for delivery of US$149 million of Egypt's debts to the airline.

Finally, they gave that paper to Dr. Shibani, the head of the central bank at the time, and he signed it. They took the paper outside the meeting and then brought it for me to do the final signature. I saw the minutes of the meeting of the board of trustees of the Foreign Exchange Reserve Account, and a figure of around 150 million dollars of currency has been allocated for the purchase of three planes. I asked Mr. Shibani, are you aware of this issue? His answer was negative. I asked why did you sign? He told me that they had said that because others had also signed. I told Mr. Shibani that this resolution had three fundamental flaws:

- First, they did not go through the expert procedures in the secretariat of the foreign exchange reserve account and they came straight to get the signatures of the members.
- Second, none of the relevant authorities and the operating bank had come to obtain this credit, and Mr. Marashi, who was a Member of the Parliament, had come to obtain this approval directly. It was not known what responsibility they had in this resolution.
- Thirdly, this credit was requested for the purchase of four second-hand airplanes with a lifespan of about 15 years, while the figure included in this resolution is the price of four almost new airplanes.

Mr. Shibani decided to cross his signature. I advised him to write an explanation above their signature instead of underlining that this resolution should be referred to the Foreign Exchange Commission and after expert review, it should be presented to the Board of Trustees. Mr. Shaibani wrote this. I also wrote sentences with the same content on the resolution and sent the paper out.

After a few minutes, Mr. Shibani was invited outside the meeting. He left and when he came back, he said that Mr. Marashi explained that these planes were almost new, but they cheated and wrote in the approval that they were manufactured 15 years ago so that they could not be subject to sanctions.

I told Mr. Shaibani that this is not possible at all. Every plane that comes out of the factory, from the first moment, all its characteristics had been recorded. Every flight it makes and every part it changes is registered to every airport it flies to. In each flight, the name and details of the pilot and his co-pilot are recorded. It is impossible to imagine buying a two-year-old plane as a 15-year-old plane. Mr. Shibani was satisfied with this explanation and the matter was postponed to expert examination. When the meeting ended, Mr. Mehdi Karbasian (Deputy General) and Mr. Meghrebein Hosseini (Deputy for Parliament Affairs) rushed to the office and said, "What are you doing?" I said nothing, I was in a government meeting, it's over, I came to the office.

They said that Mr. Marashi wrote an impeachment text in the parliament and collected more than 15 signatures and presented it to the parliament and gave a message that if he signs the resolution as he requested, he will withdraw the impeachment.

I told Mr. Karbasian to tell Mr. Marashi that this is a good opportunity to discuss the issue in the public meeting of the parliament, which will be broadcast live. I welcomed this impeachment. I told them to know that when the issue is brought up, I will explain all of its contents to the people and their representatives in the parliament completely and without prejudice. I said that the result of the impeachment was not important to me. I told him to tell his friends and party members to know and not complain later why I publicised these issues. Mr. Karbasian conveyed this message to Mr. Marashi and half an hour later, the news came that they withdrew the impeachment.

Alef newspaper,
10 March 2014

Despite all the attempts made by Tahmasb Mazaheri to offer clarity, Akbar Hashemi Rafsanjani used his influence to get approval and require all government parties to allow MMC to receive Iran's debt from Egypt in the form of three almost brand new Russian-made aircraft. Akbar Hashemi Rafsanjani later said in his memoir about the delivery of the aircraft: "In April 1993, during one of my visits from Kerman, I saw two passenger aircraft (Tu-154Ms) that Mr Seyed Hossein Marashi, governor of Kerman, had received from Egypt in exchange for that country's debt, in order to establish Mahan Air. It was an important work as we got our money and at same time we provided equipment for air transport of people in the province."

Construction Strength, Daily Diaries of Ayatollah Hashemi Rafsanjani in 1993,
printed in 2021 by Office of Knowledge of Revolution

Hossein Marashi, former vice president of the Iranian regime, later explained more about the formation of the MMC and Mahan Air:

During my time as governor, I noticed the lack of air facilities [in Kerman province]. Many times we faced problems because there was no flight, so the necessity of establishing an airline was felt. I remember people were under a lot of pressure to get plane tickets. One day I was on a mission in Tehran, there was a security problem in Kerman and I had to get to Kerman as quickly as possible, but I was delayed for 24 hours at Mehrabad airport. I said let's solve this issue independently for Kerman. However, at that time, the country was far from [considering] such ideas. During the presidency of Mr. Hashemi Rafsanjani, there was an opportunity for such ideas to be proposed.

We started with four planes. In the beginning, we had several management changes and brought in different management teams. First, Mr. Haqshanas was the CEO of the institute (MMC) and managed it. After him, we brought Mr. Hosni and gave him some shares, and he returned the shares later. Hosni was a very good pilot and manager, but he was not in harmony with the culture of Iran.

He used to say that with this chaos in Iran, I cannot run a company with order and so he resigned and left. After Hosni, Mr. Banki came. During his tenure, Mahan suffered a lot, so that it can be said that Mahan had reached the end of his activities. The activity of Mahan Air was declining when Mr. Arabnejad was introduced as the CEO of Mahan and he built Mahan Air once again.

Mahan's development in this period. Mr. Arabnejad moved very well in the direction of the company's policies, which is a detailed topic. Changing the eastern plane system to the western plane was perhaps the most important of these decisions in Mahan.

Vatan Emrooz newspaper,
24 May 2014

Tupolev Tu-154M, in service with Mahan Air from 1994 to 2006

In the 1990s, Tu-154M three-engined, medium-range, narrow-body airliners were widely operated by Mahan Air for both domestic and international flights. The first two used by the airline, 91A898 and 91A899, were delivered in 1993. Originally manufactured in 1991 for Aeroflot with CCCP-85898 and CCCP-85899 civil registration codes, they were sold to Cairo Charter and Cargo company in 1992. The aircraft received SU-OAC and SU-OAD civil registration codes in Egypt respectively and were transferred to Kerman province in 1993 and received EP-JAZ and EP-ARG civil registration codes on 1 March and 1 November 1993 respectively.

EP-JAZ and EP-ARG remained inactive in Kerman until 1994, when the airline received its Air Operators Certificate (AOC) from the Iranian Civil Aviation Organization (ICAO). Kerman became the airline's hub from where the two Tu-154Ms were used for scheduled and charter flights to three domestic and two international destinations including Zahedan, Tehran and Kish in Iran, Damascus in Syria, and Dubai in the United Arab Emirates (UAE). At the same time, a pair of Il-76TDs owned by the airline were widely used for commercial cargo to international destinations, particularly to Sharjah in the UAE.

EP-JAZ and EP-ARG remained in Mahan Air's service until March and September 2000 respectively, when they were sold to Iran's Caspian Airlines and received designations EP-CPN and EP-CPO on the civil registration codes. Caspian Airlines continued operating them with Y168 cabin configuration until 20 February 2011 when they were both grounded by the ICAO due to safety issues. EP-CPN is currently stored at Mehrabad International Airport waiting to be scrapped while EP-CPO now equips a technical training school of Saha Airlines at the 1st Tactical Fighter Base of the Iranian Air Force.

The sale of the Tu-154Ms to Caspian Airlines took place after Mahan Air began operating its first two Airbus A300B4-103s. These A300 wide-body passenger aircraft had been purchased second-hand from Thai Airways by means of Silverbird Aviation in the Seychelles. Despite having acquired the two Airbus, Mahan Air continued using Tu-154Ms until 2006. At the time, Mahan Air operated a number of other Tu-154Ms, which had been dry-leased from Russian airlines.

The first Tu-154M leased by Mahan Air was RA-85722, supplied by airline Kavminvodyavia, which had previously been leased to another Iranian airline Kish Air in 1994. The aircraft received the EP-ARH civil registration code under the Air Operator Certificate (AOC) of Mahan Air and flew for the airline until 6 October 1995. Later, the aircraft was leased by Mahan Air again, this time between September 1999 and March 2000. In that period, it flew with the EP-MAU civil registration code in Iran.

Mahan Air wet- and dry-leased ten other Tu-154Ms at various times. Some had been leased to Iran Air Tours prior to being leased to Mahan Air while others were leased to that airline after their contract with Mahan Air expired. Their construction numbers (c/ns were 92A907, 92A936, 93A946, 92A928, 89A821, 93A960, 92A932, 92A939 and 91A890 and the certificates of airworthiness and civil registration codes were EP-MHB, EP-MHD, EP-MHQ, EP-MHR, EP-MHS, EP-MHT, EP-MHV, EP-MHX and EP-MHZ from the Iranian aviation authorities during their operations in Iran.

EP-MHB was operated by Mahan Air for 18 months between November 2000 and May 2002 while EP-MHD was operated between May and December 2001; EP-MHQ was operated between November 2004 and July 2005; EP-MHR between April 2003 and November 2004; EP-MHS between December 2004 and November 2006; EP-MHT between August 2002 and April 2003; EP-MHV between January 2002 and August 2003; EP-MHX between October 2001 and June 2002; EP-MHZ between October 2001 and July 2004.

The end of Tu-154M operations

In 1998, MMC selected retired Brigadier General Hamid Arabnejad, former deputy commander of IRGCGF's 41st Sarallah Infantry Division, as chief executive officer of Mahan Air. From the beginning of his career in Mahan Air, Arabnejad realized that the operations of Tu-154Ms were not cost effective when compared with western passenger aircraft. Therefore, one of his first objectives was to procure a pair of Airbus A300B4-203s as a replacement for the two Tu-154Ms.

Tu-154M was a modernised variant of the most successful model of Tu-154 in the 1970s, the 'B'. In addition to having the stronger wings of Tu-154B, its additional fuel tanks, emergency exits, improved fuel systems, avionics, air conditioning and landing gear systems, the Tu-154M was equipped with more fuel-efficient Soloviev D-30KU-154 turbofans (compared to Kuznetsov NK-8-2U turbofans of Tu-154A/B) and had aerodynamically refined wings and fuselage with a repositioned auxiliary power unit to reduce drag, and subsequently the fuel consumption, as much as possible.

Tu-154M had double-slotted flaps instead of the triple-slotted examples of Tu-154B. These flaps had an extra 36-degree position in addition to the existing 15, 28 and 45-degree positions of Tu-154A/Bs to allow reduction of noise during the approach and to allow the crew to maintain landing speed without increasing thrust of noisy engines.

Tu-154M was equipped with a new navigation complex named Jasmin. It had an I-21 inertial navigation system, and type ABSU-154 Srs 3 automatic flight control system, which complied with ICAO Cat IIIA standards. All aircraft of this type produced since the end of the 1980s received the installation of the Jasmin navigation complex.

Maximum speed and service ceiling of Tu-154M remained the same as Tu-154B-2 at 913km/h (493 kN) and 12,100m (39,700ft) respectively. Compared to T-154B-2, several flight and performance capabilities of the aircraft had been increased; it had maximum take-off weight of 102,000 to 104,000kg (225,000 to 229,000lb), maximum range of 6,600km (3,600Nm) thanks to its increased maximum fuel capacity of 49,700 litres or 13,100 gallons (compared to 47,000 litres of the Tu-154B-2)

Despite being the best of its kind in the USSR, the Tu-154M was not cost effective. Tu-154M had a maximum passenger capacity of 180 (168 in Iran) and fuel burn of 5.5 tons per hour while an Airbus A300B4-103 equipped with two US-made General Electric CF6-50C2 turbofans had a fuel burn of 4.5 tons per hour. Each D-30KU-154 engine of the Tu-154M could produce 103 kN (23,000lbf) maximum thrust, while each CF6-50C2 had 230 kN (52,000 lbf) maximum thrust enabling an Airbus A300B4-103 to carry a maximum 345 passengers within a range of 5,375km (2,900Nm).

Despite having slightly less range compared to the Tu-154M, the Airbus A300 and later A310 were determined by Mahan Air as more efficient aircraft and this resulted in the termination of all Tu-154M operations with the airline from 2006. Another key reason behind the decision was the higher maintenance costs of the Russian aircraft and the operator's dependency on Russian aircraft manufacturing plants for the simplest maintenance jobs. Iranian aircraft repair, maintenance and overhaul centres in contract could perform all levels of maintenance on Airbus A300s and A310s.

EP-JAZ, one of the first two Tu-154Ms owned by Mahan Air landing at Dubai International Airport on 28 March 1997. (Chris Chennel)

Mahan Air leased this Tu-154M, with c/n 89A821, from airline Omskavia between 4 September 2002 and 26 November 2006. It received EP-MHS Iranian civil registration code. It is landing at Dubai International Airport on 25 March 2005. (Chris Chennel)

This Tu-154M, with c/n 93A960, was leased by Mahan Air from Omskavia between 2001 and 2003. It received EP-MHT civil registration code with Mahan Air. (Chris Doggett)

Tu-154M, with c/n 91A890, was leased by Mahan Air between 2001 and 2004. It flew for the airline in Iran with EP-MHZ civil registration code. (Bruno Geiger)

Tu-154M, with c/n 92A907, was leased by Mahan Air from Belarusian airline Belavia between 2000 and 2002. Its civil registration code was EP-MHB with Mahan Air. (Dietmar Schreiber)

Ilyushin Il-76TDs in service with Mahan Air from 1993 to 2000

Mahan Air operated two Il-76TD heavy cargo aircraft for seven years between 1993 and 2000. The aircrafts' civil registration codes were EP-JAY, with c/n 1013409297, and EP-MAH, with c/n 1023409321. They were built in 1991 and 1992 respectively following an order placed for Cairo Charter & Cargo. The Egyptian airline operated them for two years with SU-OAA and SU-OAB registration prior to delivering them to Mahan Air.

Before the rise in price of aviation fuel, Il-76MDs and Il-76TDs were widely used by Mahan Air as well as Payam Air, Aram Air and Atlas Air (three other Iranian cargo airlines) to transfer freight to other countries but mainly to Sharjah. With the increase in the price of aviation fuel by the Iranian National Oil Company in 2000, the air cargo business stopped and many Iranian cargo airlines disappeared.

Mahan Air sold its two Il-76TDs to Fars Air Qeshm, which operated them with EP-TQI and EP-TQJ civil registration codes from 2000 until 2006. These two aircraft were often chartered by the Iranian Ministry of Defence to transport weapons and ammunition to Libya, Sudan and Syria. Fars Air Qeshm sold both of the Il-76TDs to Islamic Revolutionary Guard Corps Air Force (IRGCAF), which put them into service with Pars Air with EP-PCB and EP-PCC registrations.

Pars Air used the aircraft to transfer weapons and ammunition to Syria and other countries, and after this was revealed, the airline was rebranded as Yas Air and the registration codes of the aircraft were changed to EP-GOL and EP-GOM. The US Treasury Department sanctioned the airline over its role in sending weapons for Quds Force of IRGC forcing IRGC Aerospace Force (IRGCASF) to rebrand as Pouya Air. These two Il-76TDs subsequently received new registration codes, which were EP-PUO and EP-PUS.

EP-PUS was overhauled in Moscow and had its avionic system improved to IATA standards to be able to fly in international air space while EP-PUO was de-registered and received 15-2285 military serial number in IRGCASF and was leased temporarily to Syrian Air, which used it for military purposes in 2013 and 2014, after which the aircraft was put into storage in Tehran in 2015. As of December 2022, EP-PUS had been sold to to Russia.

Above: EP-JAY, with c/n 1013409297, was one of two Il-76TDs owned by Mahan Air, which were operated between 1993 and 2000. (Christian Laugier)

Right: The front section of Mahan Air's Il-76TD with EP-JAY registration code. (Christian Laugier)

Below: EP-MAH, with c/n 1023409321, was one of two Il-76TDs owned by Mahan Air and operated between 1993 and 2000. (Christian Laugier)

Tupolev Tu-204-120s in service with Mahan Air from 2005 to 2007

Tu-204 twin-engined, medium-range, narrow-body jet airliner was the last Russian-made aircraft that Mahan Air continued operating after the end of its Tu-154M operations. Two of the five Tu-204-120s owned by Cairo Aviation (previously Cairo Charter & Cargo) were wet-leased by Mahan Air for almost two years. The aircraft were SU-EAF and SU-EAI with c/ns 1450743764027 and 1450743164025. The first was manufactured in 1997 while the latter was a 1999-built aircraft.

The SU-EAF was seen in Mahan Air's use, fully painted in Mahan's brand colours for the first time in November 2005 and remained in its use until 18 December 2006, while the SU-EAI was in service from 12 December 2005 until 20 April 2007. It remained in an overall white paint scheme without the logo and title of Mahan Air painted on it unlike SU-EAF. The aircraft were used for domestic and international flights to Bandar Abbas in south Iran, Delhi and Cochin in India and Dubai in UAE.

Tu-204-120 was a variant of the Russian-made passenger aircraft equipped with non-Russian avionics and engines. It had a pair of Rolls-Royce RB211-535E4B turbofan engines, each with thrust of 192kN (43,100lbf), which could produce more thrust than the Soloviev (now Aviadvigatel) PS90A turbofans with 157kN (35,300lbf) thrust each used on Tu-204-100/200s.

With more powerful and reliable engines, the Tu-204-120 was suitable for operations in hot Iran, particularly during the summer season. More powerful engines came at the cost of increasing fuel consumption, reducing the maximum ferry range from 4,300km (2,700 miles) in Tu-204-100 to 4,100km (2,500 miles) in Tu-204-120.

Rolls-Royce RB211-535E4B engines were also slightly heavier than their Russian rival. Each RB211-535E4B had a dry weight 3,705kg (8,169lb) while this was only 2,950kg (6,500lb) in PS90A. In addition to the heavier engines, Tu-204-120 had a maximum take-off weight of 103 tons (227,000lb), almost two tons less than Tu-204-100.

At the time of its operations in Iran, Iran Air Tours showed interest in procuring Tu-204-100 equipped with PS90 engines. An agreement was signed for procurement of ten aircraft for the airline with delivery beginning in 2009. However, its plans changed as Mahan Air decided not to operate this less profitable aircraft. After their return to Egypt, Cairo Aviation continued leasing them to various customers until 2019 when the aircraft were put in storage.

SU-EAF was one of the four Tu-204-120s operated by Cairo Aviation in the 1990s. Here it can be seen in Kyiv-Boryspil airport in 2001. (Sergey Popsuyevich)

SU-EAF, one of two Tu-204-120s leased by Mahan Air from Cairo Aviation. It can be seen landing at Dubai International Airport on 5 January 2006. (Konstantin von Wedelstaedt)

Cairo Aviation was the launch customer of Tu-204-120, receiving six of them between 1998 and 2002. Two were passenger-carrier variants with 210Y cabin configuration; SU-EAF and SU-EAI were delivered in 1998 and 1999 respectively. The other four with SU-EAG, SU-EAH, SU-EAJ and SU-EAK civil registration codes were Tu-204-120C cargo variants, which were operated by Cairo Aviation Cargo or were chartered by TNT and other cargo airlines.

Classic Airbus A300s operated by Mahan Air from 1999 to 2016

Mahan Air has operated 27 Airbus A300 wide-body passenger aircraft: eight of them have been classic variants. They were three A300B2K-3Cs with EP-MHA, EP-MHM and EP-MHP civil registration codes, one A300B4-2C with EK-30039 registration, two A300B4-103s with EP-MHE and EP-MHF civil registers, and two A300B4-203s with EP-MHL and EP-MHG civil registers. Mahan Air began using classic A300s from 2000 until 2016 when its last example was retired from service.

The first two classic Mahan Air A300s, both B4-103 variants with c/ns 35 and 55 (built in 1977 and 1978 respectively) were purchased from Silverbird Aviation in 1999. They arrived in Iran on 1 and 10 November 1999 and received the Certificate of Airworthiness from ICAO under AOC of Mahan Air in 2000. EP-MHE and EP-MHF were the registration codes which were allocated to them.

A few months later, Mahan Air purchased another A300, this time a B4-203 variant from Caribjet in Antigua and Barbuda. The aircraft with c/n 204 arrived in Iran with C24Y221 seat configuration on 4 July 2000 and shortly after received EP-MHG civil register. Before being sold to Iran, it had been leased to Pakistan International Airlines for three years and had flown there with AP-BFL civil register.

After delivery of the A300s, Mahan Air mostly used them for international flights, while the Tu-154Ms were used for domestic routes. In addition to passenger flights to Jeddah in Saudi Arabia carrying pilgrims during the Hajj pilgrimage, Istanbul in Turkey, Dubai and Sharjah in UAE, the aircraft flew to Asian and European destinations such as Bangkok in Thailand, Budapest in Hungary, Cologne and Düsseldorf in Germany, and in 2007 to Manchester in the UK. From 2008, they were mostly used for domestic flights.

Mahan Air purchased five more classic Airbus A300s in 2005 and 2006. The first was an A300B4-203, with c/n 175, built in 1982 (first flight on 2 February 1982). It was purchased from Egyptian company AMC Airlines. The aircraft with SU-BMM civil register arrived in Iran on 1 November 2005 and it received EP-MHL civil register. This 25-year-old aircraft was only used for domestic flights.

Mahan Air purchased an Airbus A300B2K-3C from bankrupt Turkish airline Saga Airlines. The aircraft TC-SGA registration code, with c/n 90, was delivered to Mehrabad International Airport on 9 May 2006. It was initially used as a source of spare parts for keeping the airline's other A300s operational, however, plans changed and the aircraft was sent to Fars Co, or Fajr Ashian Aircraft MRO Company, where it was overhauled. It received EP-MHM civil registration code.

To provide Hajj flights in 2006, and lacking Airbus aircraft, Mahan Air leased three wide-body passenger aircraft from the Air Universal at Sierra Leone and Sky Gate International Aviation at Jordan for a short period of time. They were a Lockheed L1011-1-15 TriStar with 9L-LDC registration code (and c/n 1231) and two L1011-250 TriStar with JY-SGI (and c/n 1234) and 9L-LDE (c/n 1244) registration codes. The Jordanian JY-SGI returned to its country while the two other aircraft, which received EP-LDC and EP-LDE registration codes, were stored in Mehrabad International Airport and were not flown again.

The operations of Lockheed L1011s were not profitable enough, forcing Mahan Air to expand its A300 fleet. In 2006, Mahan Air purchased three Airbus A300s by means of a front company named Blue Airways or Blue Sky in Yerevan, Armenia. Blue Sky was used by Mahan Air to circumvent US embargoes and import an A310, an A320, two Boeing 747-3B3Ms and three Boeing 747-422s. Mahan Air was about to import two more Boeing 747s but the US government prevented it from taking place. All aircraft imported by Mahan Air through Blue Sky flew with an Armenian civil register obtained from the Civil Aviation of Armenia under AOC of the airline.

The A300s that Mahan Air imported through Blue Sky in Armenia were two A300B2K-3Cs, with c/ns 160 and 244, built in 1981 and 1983 respectively, and one A300B4-2C, with c/n 239, built in 1983. The aircraft were purchased indirectly from a US-based company named Tiger Aircraft Trading Inc, unaware of the Iran link. Their Armenian civil registration codes were EK-30060, EK-30039 and EK-30044 when they arrived at Mehrabad International Airport.

To avoid breaking the cover of Blue Sky, the aircraft were leased to Mahan Air and flew in Iran with Armenian civil registers. EK-30060 and EK-30044 later received EP-MHA and EP-MHP civil registers respectively, in 2008, while EK-30039 was donated to the Iraqi government in October 2007. It was used as a VIP aircraft by the Iraqi president and was fully maintained and operated by Mahan Air helping the company and IRGC Quds Force to expand influence across the region.

During the Hajj pilgrimage of 2008, Saudi Arabian Airlines wet-leased three A300s from Mahan Air, EP-MHF, EP-MHG and EP-MHL alongside one of its two Boeing 747-3B3Ms (later registered as EP-MNE) to transport Iranian pilgrims to Saudi Arabia. Due to US sanctions, none of the above mentioned aircraft were allowed to receive fuel in Saudi airports if they were operated by Mahan Air. On 17 August 2008, EP-MHL had No.1 engine failure in Sari from where it had plans to airlift hundreds of pilgrims to Medina in Saudi Arabia forcing Saudi Arabian Airlines to send a replacement aircraft, TC-OAA, an Airbus A300-605R, leased from Turkey's Onur Air, to fulfil the service obligation.

Retirement of Mahan Air's classic A300s

In December 2022, Mahan Air had no classic Airbus A300s in service and six years had passed since the retirement of the last one of them. EP-MHE, with c/n 35, was the first to be retired in 2008, due to cracks found in the roots of its wings. The aircraft was prepared for a flight from Mehrabad

International Airport to Kerman airport where Mahan Air had planned to store it and use it as a training aid for its flight attendants. On 11 November 2008, when departing from Mehrabad, one of its two CF6-50C2 engines failed resulting in its take-off being aborted. The engine was replaced and it was flown to Kerman a few days later.

EP-MHG, an Airbus A300B4-203, was the second to be retired from service in September 2011, and was stored in Khomeini International Airport, where it was used for parts. EP-MHG and its engines were famed as troublemakers among technicians because of the multiple technical failures that they experienced during the final three years of operations. The problems included pressurisation system failure during a flight from Tehran to Kerman on 2 February 2009; engine failure during a flight from Assaluyeh to Tehran on 13 January 2010; engine failure during a flight from Mashhad to Kish on 10 December 2010; and a hydraulic system failure during a flight from Tehran to Ahvaz on 15 December 2010.

In 2013, three other classic A300s retired from service including EP-MHA, EP-MHF and EP-MHP on 5 February, 10 and 17 April respectively. EP-MHA, which was an A300B2K-3C, was flown to Kerman where it was stored, while the other two aircraft were put in storage at Khomeini International Airport. They were both cannibalised for parts to keep the last two classic A300s operated by Mahan Air in service. In December 2022, EP-MHP was still in storage in Khomeini International Airport while EP-MHF was a training aircraft for rescue simulation by the fire department at the same airport.

In May 2015, Mahan Air's A300B4-203 with registration EP-MHL, and in April 2016, A300B2K-3C, with registration EP-MHM, and c/n 90, were retired from service. Both were put in storage in Khomeini International Airport, and their engines and useful parts, which could be used on A300B4-603/605Rs were removed.

EP-MHF, with c/n 55, was one of the first two of Mahan Air's Airbus A300B4-103s. It is seen here at Mehrabad International Airport, during landing on 11 October 2010. (Babak Taghvaee)

Above: EP-MHF, with c/n 55, is seen during departure from Mehrabad International Airport, on 24 May 2013. (Babak Taghvaee)

Left: EP-MHG, an Airbus A300B4-203, with c/n 204, built in 1982, was operated by Mahan Air between 2001 and 2011. Here it can be seen at Mashhad International Airport on 6 July 2011. (Babak Taghvaee)

EP-MHL, an Airbus A300B4-203, with c/n 175, and built in 1982, was operated by Mahan Air between 2005 and 2015. Here it can be seen at Mehrabad International Airport on 6 October 2008. (Babak Taghvaee)

EP-MHL, an Airbus A300B4-203 (right) and EP-MNT, an A300B4-603 (left) can be seen in the domestic ramp of Mehrabad International Airport on 18 February 2013. (Babak Taghvaee)

EP-MHM, an Airbus A300B2K-3C, with c/n 90, and built in 1980, was operated by Mahan Air between 2006 and 2016. Here it can be seen at Mehrabad International Airport on 11 September 2012. (Babak Taghvaee)

EP-MHM, an Airbus A300B2K-3C, with c/n 90, and built in 1980, was operated by Mahan Air between 2006 and 2016. Here it can be seen at Mehrabad International Airport on 20 January 2010. (Babak Taghvaee)

EP-MHA, an Airbus A300B2K-3C, with c/n 160, and built in 1981, was operated by Mahan Air between 2006 and 2013. Here it can be seen at Mehrabad International Airport on 5 July 2011. (Babak Taghvaee)

Right: This close-up image shows CF6-80C2R turbofan engines of EP-MHA, an Airbus A300B2K-3C, with c/n 160, and built in 1981, which was operated by Mahan Air between 2006 and 2013. Here it can be seen at Mehrabad International Airport on 14 April 2009. (Babak Taghvaee)

Below: EP-MHP, an Airbus A300B2K-3C, with c/n 244, and built in 1983, was operated by Mahan Air between 2006 and 2013. Here it can be seen at Mehrabad International Airport on 3 March 2013. (Babak Taghvaee)

This close-up image shows CF6-50C2R turbofan engines of EP-MHP, an Airbus A300B2K-3C with c/n 244, and built in 1983, which was operated by Mahan Air between 2006 and 2013. Here it can be seen at Mehrabad International Airport on 27 May 2009. (Babak Taghvaee)

This Airbus A300B4-2C, with c/n 239, was operated by Mahan Air in 2006 and 2007 with EK-30039 registration code. It was donated to the Iraqi government and received YI-APX registration code. It was damaged after a rocket launched by IRGC-backed militias of Hashd Al-Shaabi hit it in Baghdad International Airport on 28 January 2022. (Babak Taghvaee)

This image shows the nose section of YI-APX, the A300B4-2C that Mahan Air donated to the Iraqi government. It can be seen during landing at Mehrabad International Airport, on 18 October 2010. (Babak Taghvaee)

Mahan Air's Botia Flight Academy: 2004 to today

On 4 October 2004, Mahan Air established its own pilot school: Botia Flight Academy at Kerman Airport. The key objective was to domestically train future commercial pilots including members of Marashi family and also to profit by training private pilots by means of a fleet of Diamond DA-40Ds and DA-42s and later Tecnam P92js light training aircraft.

In the years between 2004 and 2006, Mahan Air purchased six Diamond DA-40Ds, each equipped with a single Thielert TAE 125-01 piston engine. They are EP-BTA (c/n D4.171), EP-BTB (c/n D7.178), EP-BTC (c/n D7.179), EP-BTD (c/n D7.181), EP-BTE (c/n D7.182) and EP-BTF (c/n D7.183). Later four brand new Diamond DA-42 Twin Stars, each equipped with two Thielert TAE 125-01 engines, were purchased through an Armenian shell company and were imported for the school. They are EP-BTG (c/n 42.129), EP-BTH (c/n 42.130), EP-BTI (c/n 42.133) and EP-BTJ (c/n 42.134).

Because of sanctions and a lack of students in the school, Botia soon had most of its Diamond DA-40/42s grounded. In 2009, only two DA-40Ds and one DA-42 were active. The Thielert TAE 125-01 engines were an issue as no company in Iran was able to repair them, forcing Mahan Air to send them overseas for repair and overhaul. The Botia increased the number of its airworthy DA-40/42s in 2012. One DA-40D and one DA-42 were stationed in Payam Airport near Karaj to be used for a second branch of the flight academy near Tehran, while the other eight aircraft were kept in Kerman.

The school has lost two of its DA-40Ds in two non-fatal crashes. In February 2011, EP-BTF had an emergency landing near the city of Qazvin due to engine failure. During the emergency landing at a farm, the aircraft was heavily damaged and was later withdrawn from use. Two years later, on 5 May 2013, EP-BTA had a hard landing on a road, near the city of Kerman, after an engine failure during a solo flight of a Botia student. It was damaged and was withdrawn from use.

The high cost of maintaining DA-40/42s and difficulties in sourcing spare parts for them and their engines forced Mahan Air to buy Tecnam products as a replacement for them. Subsequently, the airline purchased four Tecnam P92js, each equipped with Rotax 912s piston engine and two Tecnam P2010s, each equipped with a Lycoming IO-360 piston engine. P92js aircraft are EP-BTK, EP-BTL, EP-BTM and EP-BTN, while P2010s are EP-BTO and EP-BTP.

Botia flight academy also has several full-motion flight simulators in Kerman, which are Airbus A300B4, A300B4-600 and RJ-70/100. Every year, Mahan Air pilots travel to Kerman Airport to fly in these simulators. In 2014, Mahan Air planned to purchase an A340 and a B744 flight simulator. In December 2022, the A340 simulator had been purchased while the plans for procurement of B744 simulators had been cancelled.

EP-BTD was one of the six DA-40Ds of Botia Flight Academy. It can be seen in Payam Airport in July 2012. (Babak Taghvaee)

Above: EP-BTJ was one of the four DA-42s of Botia Flight Academy. It can be seen in Payam Airport in July 2012. (Babak Taghvaee)

Left: EP-BTO is one of two Tecnam P2010s of Botia Flight Academy. It can be seen in the aircraft hangar of Botia in Kerman International Airport on 29 March 2017. (Frazad Farajpour)

Chapter 2
The Long-Haul Fleet Today

Mahan Air's modern A300s from 2009 to today

In 2009, Mahan Air indirectly purchased 13 of 15 Airbus A300B4-603s and 605Rs from Lufthansa, which were aged between 16 and 23 years old. Once retired from service, they were overhauled by Lufthansa Technik before being delivered to Mahan's front airline, Kyrgyz TransAvia, which procured them for Mahan Air. Five of them were flown to Iran in 2009 and another eight in 2010.

Mahan Air used these aircraft on both domestic and international routes. They fully replaced the classic A300s on their flights to European destinations in 2010 and 2011. In addition, they were used for flights to regional destinations such as Baghdad, Erbil, Dubai and Istanbul, while internationally they flew regularly to Moscow, Düsseldorf, Birmingham and Larnaca in Cyprus, as well as Almaty in Kazakhstan, and Bangkok in Thailand.

A300B4-600 aircraft were superior to classic A300s in every aspect. They were slightly longer than both A300B2s and B4s and had increased cabin space at the empennage section allowing installation of two additional rows of seats due to use of the rear fuselage of A310. They had improved wing design featuring a re-cambered trailing edge, the incorporation of simpler single-slot Fowler flaps, the deletion of slat fences, and the removal of the outboard ailerons after they were deemed unnecessary on the A310.

They also had more powerful engines compared to the CF6-50C2 and C2R of the classic A300s with maximum 51,000lbf and 53,000lbf thrust each. The ten ex-Lufthansa A300B4-603s each had a pair of CF6-80C2A3 turbofans each producing 58,500lbf thrust, while the three A300B4-605Rs each had a pair of CF6-80C2A5s producing maximum 61,500lbf maximum (take-off) thrust.

In addition to wing and fuselage design improvements, more powerful engines and a longer range due to the installation of more fuel tanks, the A300B4-600s had significantly better avionic systems allowing removal of the role of a flight engineer. Due to having more reliable and up-to-date avionics and navigation systems, they were allowed to fly within EU airspace unlike the classic Mahan Air A300s.

Out of the 13 former Lufthansa A300s that Mahan Air procured, five were delivered in 2009. Four were A300B4-603s with D-AIAN (c/n 411), D-AIAP (c/n 414), D-AIAR (c/n 546) and D-AIAS (c/n 553) registration codes and one A300BR-605R with D-AIAY (c/n 608) register had been put in storage in Dresden, Hamburg and Frankfurt since 2008. Before arriving in Iran, they were flown to Boryspil International Airport, Kyiv, where they received EX-35009, EX-35008, EX-35007, EX-35010 and EX-35006 registers under AOC of Kyrgyz TransAvia.

These aircraft with c/ns 411, 414, 546, 553 and 608 arrived at Tehran between 18 and 25 July 2009. They later received EP-MNR, EP-MNS, EP-MNT, EP-MNQ and EP-MNU civil registration codes under AOC of Mahan Air. Among these aircraft EP-MNS became a source for spare parts in 2017. After being heavily cannibalised, its wings were cut and its fuselage was stored next to Mahan Air's maintenance hangar at Khomeini International Airport in 2018. The aircraft fuselage was later burned due to an accident on 31 October 2018 and was scrapped a few days later.

In 2010, Mahan Air received the remaining eight ex-Lufthansa A300s. Six of them were A300B4-603s with D-AIAH (c/n 380), D-AIAL (c/n 405), D-AIAM (c/n 408), D-AIAT (c/n 618) and D-AIAU (c/n 623) registers and two A300B4-605Rs with D-AIAZ (c/n 701) and D-AIAX (c/n 773) civil registers. They arrived in Tehran between 30 June and 3 December 2010. They later received EP-MNJ (c/n 380), EP-MNH (c/n 405), EP-MNI (c/n 408), EP-MNK (c/n 618), EP-MNL (c/n 623), EP-MNN (c/n 701) and EP-MNM (c/n 773) civil registers.

In 2011, Mahan Air purchased five more A300-600s, one via Kyrgyz TransAvia, and the other four via Vertir Airlines based in Armenia, a front company of Mahan Air. The example imported via Kyrgyz TransAvia was an A300B4-622R, with c/n 838, and was the last A300 passenger aircraft manufactured by Airbus. It was first flown on 28 August 2002, and was delivered by Japan Air System (JAS). It arrived in Tehran with EX-35011 register of Kyrgyz TransAvia on 29 October 2011. It later received EP-MMO civil registration under AOC of Mahan Air.

The four aircraft purchased via Vertir Airlines were two A300B4-601s with c/ns 368 and 398 and two A300B4-605Rs with c/ns 464 and 518. All four were purchased from Thai Airways International. Unlike the A300B4-622R, these were cannibalised for their parts to keep the Mahan Air's fleet of A300-600s operational. These four aircraft arrived in Iran with Armenian civil registers obtained under AOC of Vertir Airlines. They were EK-30068, EK-30098, EK-30064 and EK-30018.

Current fate of the A300-600 fleet

Mahan Air retired four of its A300B4-603s between 2014 and 2020. EP-MNR was retired at Khomeini International Airport in 2014 and was later scrapped in 2020; EP-MNS was retired in 2017 and was scrapped in 2018; EP-MNK was retired on 12 May 2019 when it was flown from Tehran to Kerman for permanent storage and is now fully cannibalised for its parts; and EP-MNL was retired on 15 February 2020 after it was flown from Tehran to Kerman for permanent storage and future parts.

In December 2022, Mahan Air had ten A300-600s in operation. Four had been dry-leased to Iran Air Tours, four were under or waiting for maintenance, leaving two airworthy A300-600s in operational use. They were EP-MNJ and EP-MNH; both A300B4-603s. EP-MNJ had become operational on 25 March 2021, after a D-check following years of being kept in storage.

Flight logs of EP-MNJ in 2022 showed its use on domestic flights between Tehran, Kerman, Kish, Ahvaz, Assaluyeh, Mashhad, Bandar Abbas and Isfahan, and International flights to Baghdad and Najaf. Flight logs of EP-MNH showed its activities on domestic routes between Tehran, Kerman, Assaluyeh, Kish, Bandar Abbas, Ahvaz, Shiraz, Isfahan, Mashhad and Zahedan and also international flights to Baghdad. Both of these aircraft were often used for flights to Damascus and chartered flights to Aleppo for transportation of IRGC Quds Force personnel and their foreign proxies.

In December 2022, four other A300B4-603s with EP-MNG, EP-MNT, EP-MNQ and EP-MMO registers were in storage waiting to be repaired or were under maintenance. EP-MNG and EP-MNQ had been in storage since 2021 and 2016 respectively, while EP-MNT and EP-MMO had been waiting for C-check since 7 August 2019 and 22 May 2022 respectively.

Dry- and wet-leasing A300-600s

With the intensification of the Syrian Civil War in 2011, Mahan Air's passenger aircraft were utilised by IRGC Quds Force to transfer weapons and also members of this military organisation to various cities of Syria, particularly Damascus. This happened while IRGCASF, the Iranian Air Force and Iran Air Cargo had their heavy transport aircraft involved in such missions at that time. However, due to availability of only two Il-76TD in IRGCASF, a Boeing 747-2J9F in the IRIAF and a Boeing 747-21AC in Iran Air, IRGCQF required Mahan Air to undertake logistic support missions in Syria.

As a result of the use of Mahan Air's aircraft by the IRGCQF, the US Treasury Department sanctioned the airline in 2011. On 12 October 2011, the Treasury Department announced that it had designated the Iranian commercial airline Mahan Air pursuant to Executive Order (E.O.) 13224 for providing financial, material and technological support to the Islamic Revolutionary Guard Corps-Quds Force (IRGC-QF). Based in Tehran, according to the Treasury Department, Mahan Air had provided transportation, funds transfers and personnel travel services to the IRGC-QF.

"Mahan Air's close coordination with the IRGC-QF – secretly ferrying operatives, weapons and funds on its flights – reveals yet another facet of the IRGC's extensive infiltration of Iran's commercial sector to facilitate its support for terrorism," said Under Secretary for Terrorism and Financial Intelligence David S. Cohen on 12 October 2011. "Following the revelation about the IRGC-QF's use of the international financial system to fund its murder-for-hire plot, today's action highlights further the undeniable risks of doing business with Iran."

Later, on 19 September 2012, the US Treasury Department added 42 Mahan Air passenger aircraft into OFAC's Specially Designated Nationals and Blocked Persons' list. Among them were all Mahan Air's Airbus A300s including those procured for parts. Sanctioning the fleet made it more difficult for Mahan Air to obtain spare parts for its aircraft but also to buy fuel from any company with ties to the United States during flights to Asian and European destinations resulting in the temporary halt of some of the international flights of the airline.

It was not cost-effective for Mahan Air to use its A300B4-603/605Rs for long-distance international flights in which the aircraft needed refuelling prior to return to Iran. As a result, with the delivery of Airbus A340-311/313X long-haul aircraft, Mahan Air started using them in flights to European destinations such as Düsseldorf. With the delivery of ex-Virgin Atlantic's A340-642s, Mahan Air started operating flights to Asian destinations as well, leaving A300-600s for use on mostly domestic flights or short-range international flights.

To ensure sustainability and profitability of the A300-600 fleet, Mahan Air's managers decided to dry- or wet-lease them to various airlines. Following an intergovernmental agreement between Iran and Syria, Mahan Air was tasked to undertake responsibility for maintenance and overhaul of Airbus A320 CEO fleet of Syrian Air and also to equip the airline with wide-body and long-range passenger aircraft to establish international flights to Middle Eastern destinations. Subsequently, in 2016, Mahan Air's A300B4-605R, with EP-MNM civil registration, was delivered to Syrian Air and was operated by that company between 4 August 2016 and 15 March 2017, when it was replaced by an Airbus A340-313X, with YK-AZA register.

In 2015, Mahan Air established a front airline named Tehran Air in order to operate some of its Airbus A310s and A300s as well as RJ85/100s for domestic and international use and also to procure Airbus A319s and A320s for Mahan Air. Before starting operations, information about Tehran Air's ties to Mahan Air was leaked resulting in termination of the plan. Mahan Air managed to purchase five Airbus A319-111/112s, which entered service with Mahan Air but were never operated by the airline. Three were sold to Iran Air while two were sold to Meraj Air in 2019.

Back in 2018, Mahan Air reached an agreement with Iran Air Tours through which it began leasing its aircraft to the airline. It was started with EP-MNN, one of three of Mahan Air's A300B4-605Rs. It was in storage for years before overhaul and delivery to Iran Air Tours on 29 October 2018. The aircraft received EP-MDN registration under AOC of Iran Air Tours in November 2019. The next aircraft after EP-MNN was another A300B4-605R with EP-MNM civil register. Mahan Air began operating the aircraft from 10 March 2019 after its C-check. The aircraft later received EP-MDM registration code under AOC of Iran Air Tours in June 2020.

EP-MNI, an A300B4-603 and EP-MNU, the third of Mahan Air's A300B4-605R, were sold to Iran Air Tours and were put into operation from 14 August 2019 and 14 May 2020 respectively. EP-MNU's register was later changed to EP-MDU on 11 April 2021. In December 2021, Mahan Air had its two A310s purchased through Armenia Airways in 2018 passed to Iran Air Tours. They received EP-MDK and EP-MDL civil registers.

Above: EP-MMO (c/n 838) is the sole Mahan Air Airbus A300B4-622R and has been in service since 2013. It is seen at Mehrabad International Airport on 8 July 2013. (Babak Taghvaee)

Left: EP-MNG (c/n 401) is Mahan Air's A300B4-603 and has been in service since 2010. It is seen at Mashhad International Airport on 5 July 2011. (Babak Taghvaee)

Flight crew of EP-MNH (c/n 405), Mahan Air's A300B4-603 has been in service since 2010. It is seen at Kerman International Airport in 2011. (Mahan Air)

EP-MNH (c/n 405), Mahan Air's A300B4-603 has been in service since 2010. It can be seen at Mehrabad International Airport on 4 December 2010. (Babak Taghvaee)

EP-MNI (c/n 408), Mahan Air's A300B4-603 has been in service since 2010. It is seen at Mehrabad International Airport on 3 March 2013. (Babak Taghvaee)

EP-MNI (c/n 408), Mahan Air's A300B4-603 has been in service since 2010. It is seen at Mehrabad International Airport on 1 September 2012. (Babak Taghvaee)

EP-MNI (c/n 408), Mahan Air's A300B4-603 is seen in use by Iran Air Tours at Zahedan International Airport on 28 April 2017. (Ahmad Mahgoli)

EP-MNJ (c/n 380), Mahan Air's A300B4-603 has been in service since 2010. It is seen at Mehrabad International Airport on 18 January 2012. (Babak Taghvaee)

EP-MNK (c/n 618), Mahan Air's A300B4-603 has been in service since 2010. It is seen at Mehrabad International Airport on 17 March 2011. (Babak Taghvaee)

EP-MNK (c/n 618), Mahan Air's A300B4-603 has been in service since 2010. It is seen at Mehrabad International Airport on 20 May 2012. (Babak Taghvaee)

EP-MNL (c/n 623), Mahan Air's A300B4-603, in service between 2010 and 2020, is seen inside its maintenance hangar at Khomeini International Airport on 17 October 2010. (Alireza Mahan)

EP-MNL (c/n 623), a retired Mahan Air A300B4-603, is in use as fire trainer at Kerman Airport. (Samira Ramezani)

EP-MNM (c/n 773) is Mahan Air's A300B4-605R and has been in service since 2010. It is seen in use by Syrian Air at Damascus International Airport in 2016. (Author's collection)

EP-MNM (c/n 773) is Mahan Air's A300B4-605R, in service since 2010. It is seen at Mehrabad International Airport on 23 August 2013. (Babak Taghvaee)

EP-MNN (c/n 701) is Mahan Air's A300B4-605R, in service since 2010. It is seen at Mehrabad International Airport on 10 July 2011. (Babak Taghvaee)

EP-MNQ (c/n 553) is Mahan Air's A300B4-603 in service since 2010. It is seen at Mehrabad International Airport on 27 January 2010. (Babak Taghvaee)

EP-MNQ (c/n 553) is Mahan Air's A300B4-603 in service since 2010. It is seen at Mehrabad International Airport on 30 August 2012. (Babak Taghvaee)

EP-MNR (c/n 411) is Mahan Air's A300B4-603 and has been in service since 2009. It is seen at Mehrabad International Airport on 12 March 2012. (Babak Taghvaee)

EP-MNS (c/n 414) is Mahan Air's A300B4-603 in service since 2009. It is seen at Mehrabad International Airport on 15 December 2009. (Babak Taghvaee)

EP-MNT (c/n 546) is Mahan Air's A300B4-603 in service since 2009. It is seen at Mehrabad International Airport, Tehran on 18 July 2009. (Babak Taghvaee)

EP-MNT (c/n 546) is Mahan Air's A300B4-603 in service since 2009. It is being overhauled at Fars Co or Fajr Ashian Aircraft MRO Centre, Tehran, on 7 January 2018. (Ali Naderi)

EP-MNU (c/n 608) is Mahan Air's A300B4-605R in service since 2009. It is seen at Mehrabad International Airport on 12 August 2013. (Babak Taghvaee)

EP-MDU (c/n 608) is an A300B4-605R, which was in use by Mahan Air as EP-MNU. It is seen at Khomeini International Airport in September 2021. (Keyvan Tavakkoli)

Before changing its serial number to EP-MDU, Mahan Air's A300B4-605R, with c/n 608, and leased to Iran Air Tours still carried the EP-MNU registration code as can be seen here at Zahedan International Airport on 29 June 2020. (Ahmad Mahgoli)

EP-MNU (c/n 608) is Mahan Air's A300B4-605R in service since 2009. It is seen at Mehrabad International Airport on 12 August 2013. (Babak Taghvaee)

EK-30068, an A300B4-601 previously used by Thai Airways was purchased by Mahan Air for spare parts in 2010. It can be seen in use as a fire trainer in Khomeini International Airport in August 2012. (Babak Taghvaee)

Mahan Air's Airbus A310s from 2002 to today

Mahan Air currently operates 12 Airbus A310-304, 308, 324 and 325 wide-body passenger aircraft, which play an important role delivering flights to international and regional destinations, in particular Syria and Lebanon. With slightly longer range and flight endurance when compared to the A300-600s, they have enabled Mahan Air to fly as far as Kuala Lumpur, Malaysia, and also to Europe without any need to refuel at the destination.

The A300-600 has a typical seating arrangement, fitting between 247 and 345 passengers in a three-class layout, while A310-300 can carry between 220 and 275 passengers. An A300-600 may carry 22 LD3 containers in the lower deck while the A310-300 may carry a maximum of 14.

The A310-304, when equipped with a pair of GE CF6-80C2A2s engines and the A310-308 when equipped with two GE CF6-80C2A8s engines have a maximum take-off weight of 153,000kg and 164,000kg respectively. They both have a maximum range of 9,600km without payload and 5,600km with maximum payload. The GE CF6-80C2A2 engines of the A310-304 can produce a maximum 53,200lbf thrust each, while the GE CF6-80C2A8 engines can produce a maximum 59,000lbf thrust each. The former has a fuel burn of 4,400kg per hour while the latter has a fuel burn of 4,300kg per hour.

In the years between 2002 and 2019, Mahan Air purchased 11 Airbus A310-304s, one A310-308, two A310-324s and two A310-325s. Fourteen of these aircraft were purchased by Mahan Air's front companies to circumvent US embargoes on the Iranian aviation industry. The front airlines and companies used to purchase these aircraft were Asia Sky Lines in Tajikistan, Armenia Airlines in Armenia, Blue Sky in Armenia, Kyrgyz Trans Avia in Tajikistan, Vertir Airlines in Armenia, and Zarand in France.

Included were a pair of A310-304s from Turkish Airlines with TC-JDC (c/n 537) and TC-JDD (c/n 586) civil registers, which were purchased through loans that Zarand obtained from a French bank. After arriving in Iran on 1 June and 7 August 2002, they received EP-MHI and EP-MHH civil registers respectively. EP-MHH was quickly put into operation in June 2002 and was used for international flights to Istanbul, Birmingham, Düsseldorf, Bangkok as well as domestic flights. EP-MHI was put into operation from June 2003 and flew to similar destinations.

EP-MHI and EP-MHH registers were changed to F-OJHI and F-OJHH civil registers respectively under the AOC of Mahan's front company in France in July 2004. Under cover of being leased from Zarand Investment Company, they could fly to destinations where the US government prohibited Mahan Air to to fly to until September 2012. The aircraft were put in storage in 2012. In May 2015, Mahan began using F-OJHH with a new register, EP-MMP, after it was fully overhauled using parts of now retired EP-MHI.

To reduce the pressure on its two A310-304s, Mahan Air dry-leased an A310-304 with TC-SGC civil register from Saga Airlines, in Turkey, for ten months in 2005. The aircraft arrived in Tehran on 17 December 2005 and left Iran in October 2006 just before Mahan Air began using its third A310. Later in 2012, Iran Air Tours purchased TC-SGC, which arrived at Mashhad on 28 September 2012 but because several key documents related to the aircraft's operations were missing, Iran's Civil Aviation Organization refused to issue a certificate of airworthiness for the aircraft. A few weeks later, Mahan Air purchased the aircraft and cannibalised it to use its parts on its other aircraft in 2012.

On 12 December 2006, the third A310-304 entered Iran. It was previously in service with Lufthansa (until 2003) and then global container shipping line Hapag-Lloyd (until 2006). Mahan Air procured this 17-year-old aircraft through Kyrgyz TransAvia. The aircraft was operated with EX-301 Kyrgyz registration code by Mahan Air until November 2013 when it was changed to

EP-MMN. It was used by Mahan Air for international flights to Bangkok until 2008 and then was mostly used for domestic flights.

The fourth Mahan Air A310-304, with c/n 488, was built in 1989 and previously used by Lufthansa and Hapag-Lloyd, entered Iran on 16 January 2007. It was purchased by Blue Sky in Armenia, and flew for the airline with an Armenian registration of EK-31088 until May 2008 when it received EP-MHO register under AOC of Mahan Air. It flew for the airline with a C12 Y210 seating configuration until 16 July 2022.

In 2008, Mahan Air purchased three more A310s through Kyrgyz TransAvia. The aircraft with c/ns 564, 567 and 620 arrived in Iran with EX-35005, EX-35003 and EX-35004 registration codes. The first two had been used by CSA Czech Airlines while the third was operated by Hapag-Lloyd until 2008. EX-35003 (A310-304) and EX-35004 (A310-308) arrived at Tehran on 21 and 29 December 2008 respectively, while the third aircraft (A310-304) arrived on 25 June 2009. They received EP-MNN, EP-MNP and EP-MNX civil registers under AOC of Mahan Air in 2009 and 2010. They were used by Mahan for both domestic and international flights and often flew to Dubai, Phuket, Guangzhou, Istanbul, Milan and Düsseldorf.

In 2010, Mahan Air used Vertir Airlines in Armenia to purchase two A310-304s. The aircraft with c/ns 547 and 595 were operated by Canadian Air Transat with C-GTSD and C-GTSI civil registers respectively, between 2004 and 2009. The first arrived in Tehran with the EK-31095 register of Vertir Airlines on 28 January 2010, while the other arrived with EK-31047 register on 9 April 2011. EK-31095 was initially used by Mahan for spare parts for EP-MNN until May 2012, after which it was used by the airline for passenger flights with EP-MNO register following an overhaul. EK-31047 followed a similar fate for two years until it entered Mahan Air's service with EP-MNF civil register and C24 Y164 seating configuration.

In 2011, Mahan Air purchased a German Air Force A310-304 with c/n 499, 10+22 serial number and 'Theodor Heuss' fleet name. The aircraft was in use for VIP flights by German government authorities from August 1991. A group of Ukrainian businessmen purchased the aircraft for Mahan Air for €3.1 million. It was flown to Boryspil airport, Kyiv, on 21 July 2011 and then to Tehran on 18 November 2011. It received an EP-VIP register as Mahan had planned to provide it for use of Iranian government officials but only succeeded in doing that twice. In 2014, Quds Force of IRGC also used it twice for flights to Sanaa, Yemen, before the aircraft was put into storage in 2015. It is now a source of spare parts for other Mahan Air A310s.

On 30 November 2014, Mahan Air began operating its twelfth A310-304. It was an A310-304 with c/n 526, built in 1989 for Lufthansa. Mahan Air purchased it from MIAT Mongolian Airlines. The airline had operated it from 2008 with JU-1010 civil register and 'Chinggis Khaan' fleet name until 2011, when it was retired. The aircraft had 56,276 hours total time and 14,283 total flight time. It arrived at Tehran on 27 July 2014, and after receiving the EP-MMJ civil register, was put into operation in November 2015.

In 2018, Mahan Air used Armenia Airways to purchase two A310-325s from a Romanian company named Tarom. These aircraft, with c/ns 636 and 644, had Pratt & Whitney PW4156A turbofan engines each capable of producing 56,000lbf thrust. The aircraft, with EK-31001 and EK-31002 registration codes, arrived at Mehrabad International Airport on 28 August 2018.

When news about the purchase of the aircraft broke, the US State Department launched an investigation about the sale to Iran of two Airbus A310-325s owned by Tarom by means of Armenia Airways to Mahan Air, resulting in their being grounded. Mahan Air returned EK-31002 to Yerevan on 16 April 2019. The aircraft was flown back to Tehran on 23 January 2020. Mahan Air later leased both aircraft to Iran Air Tours, and they have now received EP-MDK and EP-MDL civil registers.

In 2019, Mahan Air purchased its two last A310s through Asia Sky Lines in Tajikistan. They were both A310-324s equipped with Pratt & Whitney PW4152 turbofans. The first, built in 1991, with c/n 574 was operated by Uzbekistan Airways as UK-31002, and the second, built in 1998, with c/n 706, was operated by them as UK-31003. These two aircraft arrived at Mehrabad International Airport on 2 November 2019. They were planned to be operated by a new airline named Tous Airways, officially registered in Kish Island in 2019, but were not taken up, so Mahan Air began operating them with EP-MEC and EP-MED civil registers.

As of December 2022, Mahan Air had retired two of its A310 (EP-MHI and EP-MHO), two other aircraft had been cannibalised for their parts (EP-MMX and EP-MHI), two A310-325s were dry-leased to Iran Air Tours, leaving eleven A310s still in service of the airline. Among them four were under maintenance — EP-MMX, EP-MMN, EP-MNO and EP-MNP; while seven A310s with EP-MMJ, EP-MNF, EP-MNX, EP-MNV, EP-MEC, EP-MED and EP-MMP registration codes were airworthy.

Two of them, EP-MEC and EP-MMP, were mostly used for domestic flights between Ahvaz, Assaluyeh, Bandar Abbas, Kish (Island), Kerman, Mashhad and Tehran, while the others were used mostly for international flights to Erbil, Ankara, Aleppo, Baghdad, Beirut, Belgrade, Delhi, Dubai, Damascus, Istanbul, Kabul, Lahore, Moscow, St. Petersburg and Sulaimaniyah.

Chartering Mahan Air's aircraft by the Quds Force

Ex-German Air Force's A310-304, which Mahan Air purchased, was transferred to FarsCo Aircraft MRO Centre where it passed an overhaul before entering Mahan Air's service with EP-MMX civil register from 17 March 2014. It was used by the Nuclear Negotiating Team of Iran's government headed by Foreign Minister Javad Zarif, for flight to Geneva. EP-MMX was used by former President Hasan Rouhani for a flight to China on 20 May 2014.

Equipped with extra fuel tanks in its cargo hold, the EP-MMX had longer range than all the other Mahan Air A310s making it suitable for IRGCQF to charter it for direct flight to Sanaa, Yemen. It was flown to Yemen for the first time on 20 February 2015 when it transferred IRGCQF commanders and officers and evacuated several injured Houthi rebels and officials.

On 28 April 2015, this aircraft was intercepted by a pair of Royal Saudi Air Force's (RSAF) F-15C Eagle fighter jets. One of the F-15 pilots warned the A310's pilot Behzad Sedaghat-Nia, and ordered him to avoid flying to Sanaa. However, Sedaghat-Nia refused forcing the RSAF to bomb the control tower and runways of Sanaa airport to prevent the aircraft from landing. Not being able to use it for flights to Yemen, EP-MMX was of no use to the IRGCQF, and Mahan Air stored the aircraft and used it for its parts.

In November 2021, the group 'Hooshyarane Vatan', which is believed to be contracted by Israeli intelligence (Mossad) hacked Mahan Air's emails. Hackers obtained documents showing how Quds Force of IRGC was using Mahan Air's A310s to transport its personnel and foreign proxies, such as members of Hezbollah, from Tehran to Aleppo and Damascus in Syria and Beirut in Lebanon.

According to the documents, a travel agency named 'Hamrah Seir', under the management of retired Brigadier Ali-Naqi Golparast, had responsibility for ticketing for IRGCQF personnel and their proxies. With the help of a front travel agency, IRGCQF could protect the identity of its personnel and foreign proxies flying to Syria and Lebanon on flights fully chartered by the military force. According to the documents, three A310s with EP-MNO, EP-MNV and EP-MMJ civil registers were chartered by Mahan Air. These three aircraft could carry a maximum 167, 174 and 193 passengers respectively.

On 23 July 2020, one of Mahan Air's A310s, which was fully chartered by IRGC Quds Force, carrying its personnel and their families to Beirut, was intercepted by two F-15C Eagle Air superiority fighter jets of the United States Air Force's (USAF) 44th Fighter Squadron after it flew directly over a US military camp in the Al-Tanf region of Syria. The aircraft with EP-MNF register flying with W51152 / IRM1152 flight number also had several personnel of the Iranian Foreign Ministry and their relatives onboard.

Due to the presence of Quds Force personnel on board and the pilot's fear of being forced to fly to Saudi Arabia for inspection at Prince Sultan Air Base, he carried out an evasive manoeuvre after seeing the F-15Cs flying close to the aircraft. Due to a fast descent, which the pilot claimed was to avoid collision with one of the F-15Cs, several people on board were injured because they weren't wearing seatbelts at the time of the incident. According to US CENTCOM, the F-15Cs left after visually inspecting the A310 from 1,000 metres away and the EP-MNF continued its flight to Beirut.

In December 2020, Amir Asadollahi, one of Mahan's pilots revealed that once in 2013, he was carrying 200 passengers and seven tons of weapons and ammunition from Tehran to Damascus. On request of the US authorities, the Iraqi government ordered the aircraft to land in Baghdad for inspection. One of the passengers of the aircraft was Qasem Soleimani, former commander of IRGCQF. To avoid his arrest, Asadollahi told Soleimani to get into the flight deck and wear a flight engineer's uniform in order to hide his identity. When Iraqi police entered the aircraft for inspection, one of the crew members bribed them not to look at the cockpit where Qasem Soleimani was hiding.

F-OJHI or EP-MHI (c/n 537), a A310-304(ET) was used by Mahan Air between 2004 and 2012. It is seen at Mehrabad International Airport on 15 December 2008. (Babak Taghvaee)

EP-MHO (c/n 488), a A310-304 used by Mahan Air between 2006 and 2020. It is seen at Mehrabad International Airport on 23 February 2009. (Babak Taghvaee)

EX-301/EP-MMN (c/n 488), a A310-304 used by Mahan Air between 2006 and 2018. It is seen at Mehrabad International Airport on 1 September 2012. (Babak Taghvaee)

EX-301/EP-MMN (c/n 488), a A310-304 used by Mahan Air between 2006 and 2018. It is seen at Mehrabad International Airport on 1 August 2013. (Babak Taghvaee)

EX-301/EP-MMN (c/n 488), a A310-304 used by Mahan Air between 2006 and 2018. It is seen at Mehrabad International Airport on 19 June 2013. (Babak Taghvaee)

The Long-Haul Fleet Today

EP-MMX (c/n 499), an A310-304 (ET) was used by the German government as VIP aircraft until it was purchased by Mahan Air. It is seen at Mehrabad International Airport in 2016. (Tara Afshari)

EP-MNO (c/n 595), an A310-308 was used by Mahan Air between 2006 and 2018. It is seen at Mehrabad International Airport on 4 December 2010. (Babak Taghvaee)

EP-MNP (c/n 586), an A310-308 has been operated by Mahan Air since 2009. Equipped with two General Electric CF6-80C2A2 turbofan engines, it can be seen at Mehrabad International Airport on 11 April 2011. (Babak Taghvaee)

EP-MNP (c/n 586), an A310-308 operated by Mahan Air since 2009. It is seen at Mashhad International Airport on 4 July 2011. (Babak Taghvaee)

EP-MNV (c/n 567), an A310-304(ET) has been operated by Mahan Air since 2009. It is seen at Mashhad International Airport on 4 November 2010. (Babak Taghvaee)

EP-MNX (c/n 564), an A310-304(ET) has been operated by Mahan Air since 2009. It is seen at Mashhad International Airport on 4 January 2010. (Babak Taghvaee)

EP-MNX (c/n 564), an A310-304(ET) has been operated by Mahan Air since 2009. It is seen at Istanbul International Airport in September 2021. (Mahan Air)

EP-MNX (c/n 564), an A310-304(ET) has been operated by Mahan Air since 2009. It is seen departing Mehrabad International Airport on 23 August 2013. (Mahan Air)

In August 2019, the Israeli Defence Force killed two drone operators of Hezbollah, Hassem Yusuf Zabib and Yasser Ahmad Tzahar. These images taken during their flights between Tehran and Beirut were leaked indicating the use of Mahan Air aircraft by IRGCQF proxies. (Author's collection)

This document shows procurement of 1,093 tickets by IRGCQF for nine A310 flights between Tehran and Damascus between 28 March and 18 April 2021. The aircraft involved were three A310-304/308s with EP-MNO, EP-MNV and EP-MMJ registration codes. (Author's collection)

Row	Date	Row Weekday	Description	Debit
1	1400/01/08	Sunday	CHARTER FLIGHT IKA - DAM - IKA A/C MNV (174 SEAT) (PER SEAT 42.000.000	7,308,000,000
2	1400/01/08	Sunday	7 PAX OVER FOR ROUTE DAM – IKA DATE 2021/03/28	147,000,000
3	1400/01/12	Thursday	CHARTER FLIGHT IKA - DAM - IKA A/C MNO (167 SEAT) (PER SEAT	7,014,000,000
4	1400/01/15	Sunday	CHARTER FLIGHT IKA - DAM - IKA A/C MNV (174 SEAT) (PER SEAT 42.000.000	7,308,000,000
5	1400/01/15	Sunday	8 PAX OVER FOR ROUTE DAM – IKA DATE 2021/04/04	168,000,000
6	1400/01/22	Sunday	CHARTER FLIGHT IKA - DAM - IKA A/C MMJ (193 SEAT) (PER SEAT 42.000.000	8,106,000,000
7	1400/01/22	Sunday	10 PAX OVER FOR ROUTE DAM - IKA DATE 2021/04/11	210,000,000
8	1400/01/26	Thursday	CHARTER FLIGHT IKA - DAM - IKA A/C MMJ (193 SEAT) (PER SEAT 42.000.000	8,106,000,000
9	1400/01/29	Sunday	CHARTER FLIGHT IKA - DAM - IKA A/C MNO (167 SEAT) (PER SEAT	7,014,000,000
				45,381,000,000

Row	Date	Row Weekday	Description	Debit
1	1399/11/05	Sunday	CHARTER FLIGHT IKA - DAM - IKA A/C MMJ (197 SEAT) (PER SEAT 38.640.000 IRR)	7,612,080,000
2	1399/11/05	Sunday	9 PAX OVER FOR ROUTE DAM - IKA DATE 2021/01/24	173,880,000
3	1399/11/12	Sunday	CHARTER FLIGHT IKA - DAM - IKA A/C MMJ (195 SEAT) (PER SEAT 38.640.000 IRR)	7,534,800,000
4	1399/11/19	Sunday	CHARTER FLIGHT IKA - DAM- IKA A/C MMJ (195 SEAT) (PER SEAT 38.640.000 IRR)	7,534,800,000
5	1399/11/19	Sunday	4 PAX OVER FOR ROUTE DAM - IKA DATE 2021/02/07	77,280,000
6	1399/11/26	Sunday	CHARTER FLIGHT IKA - DAM - IKA A/C MMJ (195 SEAT) (PER SEAT 38.640.000 IRR)	7,534,800,000
7	1399/11/30	Thursday	CHARTER FLIGHT IKA - DAM - IKA A/C MNV (174 SEAT) (PER SEAT 38.640.000 IRR)	6,723,360,000
				37,191,000,000

This document shows procurement of 969 tickets by IRGCQF for seven A310 flights between Tehran and Damascus between 24 January and 18 February 2021. The aircraft involved were two A310-304s with EP-MNV and EP-MMJ registration codes. (Author's collection)

This document shows procurement of 730 tickets by IRGCQF for six A310 flights between Tehran and Damascus between 25 April and 16 May 2021. The aircraft involved were three A310-304/308s with EP-MNO, EP-MNV and EP-MMJ registration codes. (Author's collection)

Row	Date	Row Weekday	Description	Debit
1	1400/02/05	Sunday	CHARTER FLIGHT IKA - DAM - IKA A/C MNO (167 SEAT) (PER SEAT 42.000.000 IRR)	7,014,000,000
2	1400/02/05	Sunday	8 PAX OVER FOR ROUTE IKA - DAM DATE 2021/04/25	168,000,000
3	1400/02/12	Sunday	CHARTER FLIGHT IKA - DAM - IKA A/C MMJ (193 SEAT) (PER SEAT 42.000.000 IRR)	8,106,000,000
4	1400/02/19	Sunday	CHARTER FLIGHT IKA - DAM - IKA A/C MNV (180 SEAT) (PER SEAT 42.000.000 IRR)	7,560,000,000
5	1400/02/26	Sunday	CHARTER FLIGHT IKA - DAM - IKA A/C MNV (174 SEAT) (PER SEAT 42.000.000 IRR)	7,308,000,000
6	1400/02/26	Sunday	8 PAX OVER FOR ROUTE DAM - IKA DATE 2021/05/16	168,000,000
				30,324,000,000

Mahan Air's Airbus A340s from 2002 to today

Between 2012 and 2017, Mahan Air purchased 14 Airbus A340 long-range, wide-body passenger airliners in three different variants. They were two A340-311s each with four CFM International CFM56-5C2 turbofans, four A340-313Xs each with four CFM56-5C4 turbofans, and seven A34-642s each with four Rolls-Royce Trent 556-61 turbofans.

Two of the A340-313Xs were leased to Syrian Air in 2017 while the rest entered service with Mahan Air and carried out flights that the two Boeing 747-3B3M and three Boeing 747-422 wide-body passenger aircraft it purchased second-hand in 2006 and 2007 could not deliver. These aircraft currently fly to China, Thailand, Venezuela and other countries where refuelling in the destination country is not necessary.

The first two A340s that Mahan Air procured were ex-Lufthansa examples equipped with CFM56-5C2 engines. These two aircraft, both A340-311 models were procured through two companies. Their engines and other parts were US-made and subject to the sanctions of the US Treasury Department. The aircraft with D-AIGA (c/n 20) and D-AIGK (c/n 56) registers were first purchased by a Thai company Chaba Airlines and both were transferred to Bangkok and received HS-CHA and HS-CHB registration codes there before being transferred to a Kyrgyz company named Manas Airways on 6 October 2012.

The two A340-311s were later transferred to Kyrgyzstan where they received EX-34001 and EX-34002 Kyrgyz registration codes and from there were flown to Imam Khomeini City Airport on 22 and 26 December 2012 respectively. They were delivered with F8C48Y160 cabin configuration. A few weeks after their delivery, they received EP-MMA and EP-MMB civil registration codes under AOC of Mahan Air on 20 January 2013.

Two years later, Mahan Air purchased a third Airbus A340, this time a 313X series equipped with more powerful engines, increased maximum take-off weight of up to 275 tonnes (606,000lb). Thanks to the extra fuel tanks, the aircraft can fly a maximum of 7,200 to 7,400 nautical miles (13,300 to 13,700km) depending on the size of cargo carried and number of passengers onboard (usually 295).

At the time of procurement, the aircraft, which had previously been used by Singapore Airlines was 15 years old. It had been flown by the airline for four years until it was sold to Boeing Aircraft Holding Company in October 2003, which had leased it to Gulf Air for nine years until it was chosen by Mahan Air. It was first purchased via Falak Aviation in Johannesburg on 6 February 2014 and transferred to Manas Airways in Kyrgyzstan. While it was flying with EX-34004 registration code to Bishkek, it declared an emergency landing and landed at Khomeini International Airport on 25 July 2014. Mahan Air received EP-MMC civil registration for this aircraft on 21 August 2014.

Thanks to its extended range, EP-MMC was used by the former president of the Iranian regime, Hasan Rouhani to travel to New York, US, to give a speech during the annual debate of the UN's 69th General Assembly on 22 September 2014. The aircraft flew for 9,832km in 13 hours and 3 minutes to reach John F. Kennedy airport in New York. The Iranian government delegation used EP-MMC to travel from New York to Astrakhan in Russia on 28 September 2014. The aircraft with IRM133 call-sign carried Rouhani to Russia to attend the fourth Caspian Summit that was held on 29 September 2022. After returning to Tehran, EP-MMC was put into regular passenger operations flying to Düsseldorf.

Expanding the A340 fleet with Al-Naser Airlines

As the US government led by President Barack Obama refused to provide military support for Iraq during the first months of the Islamic State's (ISIL) rise in Iraq, Baghdad sought help from its eastern neighbour, Iran, to counter ISIL, in June 2014. Subsequently, IRGC supplied the Iraqi Armed Forces with Su-25 ground-attack fighter jets and other weapons. Its IRGC Quds Force sent advisors and troops to Iraq in order to organise Popular Mobilization Forces and use them against Daesh and ISIL. They also transferred a significant amount of weapons and ammunition to Iraq to be used by the newly formed Popular Mobilisation Units (PMU) as well as Kurdish regional government against ISIL/Daesh between June and October 2014.

Mahan Air took advantage of the improvement of the Tehran-Baghdad relationship over Iran's military support from Iraq during the war on ISIL. The Iraqi government now refused US orders to inspect

Mahan Air's cargo and passenger flights and Pouya Air's flights to Damascus. It also enabled Mahan Air to establish Al-Naser Airlines in order to procure eight Airbus A340 passenger aircraft to carry passengers including IRGCQF and PMU members inside Iraq with a single RJ100 regional passenger aircraft.

Through the Al-Naser Airlines, Mahan Air purchased one Airbus A340-313X and seven Airbus A340-642 that had been previously used by Virgin Atlantic and had just recently been retired. The A340-313X was G-VAIR 'Maiden Tokyo' (c/n 164). The aircraft had been overhauled and its cabin configuration had changed into F8C48Y160 at Tarbes-Lourdes-Pyrenees airport of France between April and July 2014. This aircraft was flown to Baghdad International Airport after its purchase by Al-Naser on 23 December 2014.

The seven other aircraft purchased by means of Al-Naser were all A340-642, which once flew for Virgin Atlantic Airways. They were G-VGOA 'Indian Princess' (c/n 371), G-VATL 'Miss Kitty' (c/n 376), G-VSHY 'Madame Butterfly' (c/n 383), G-VMEG 'Mystic Maiden' (c/n 391), G-VOGE 'Cover Girl' (c/n 416), G-VFOX 'Silver Lady' (c/n 449) and G-VSSH 'Sweet Dreamer' (c/n 615). Most of them were procured by Al-Naser from Hi Fly Malta. These seven aircraft were transferred to Baghdad and Basra between 30 July 2014 and 25 March 2015. They received YI-NAA to YI-NAG civil registers in Iraq.

The US government put pressure on the Iraqi government not to let Mahan Air transfer the eight aircraft to Iran in 2015. Due to US pressures, Iraqi officials prevented their transfer forcing the CEO of the airline, Arabnejad, to travel to Baghdad to negotiate with Iraqi officials through IRGCQF channels. He was arrested on the request of the US government but was later released with the help of General Qasem Soleimani, commander of Quds Force at that time. Arabnejad's efforts finally bore fruit and all eight A340s were released and allowed to fly to Iran on 8 May 2015.

A few weeks after their delivery, these seven aircraft with C45Y263 cabin configuration received Iranian registration codes. The A340-313X received EP-MMD register while the A340-642s became EP-MME, EP-MMF, EP-MMG, EP-MMH, EP-MMI, EP-MMR and EP-MMQ civil registers. They were used for flights to Asian and European destinations and thanks to their 7,800nm (14,446km) range, they didn't need refuelling in Europe since oil companies refused to sell aviation fuel to the airline due to the US sanctions.

COVID-19 in Iran

Mahan Air relied heavily on its A340-313Xs and 642s for flights to European destinations alongside the A310-313s. However, this didn't last long. The US government, during Donald Trump's presidency put pressure on EU governments to prevent Mahan Air's flights to their countries between April 2019 and March 2020.

Subsequently Mahan Air, which used its A340s in flights to Athens, Barcelona, Belgrade, Copenhagen, Düsseldorf, Paris, Munich, Madrid, Milan, and Rome faced a new challenge, forcing it to find a new use for its large fleet of A340s. As a result, the airline increased its flights to St Petersburg and Moscow in Russia, Bangkok in Thailand, and Beijing, Guangzhou, Shanghai and Shenzhen in China.

Thanks to the relatively cheaper aviation fuel in Iran, the airline could sell tickets cheaper than other airlines to the Middle East, drawing Chinese and Russian passengers to its transit flights to Tehran. By means of these A340s, Mahan Air also airlifted significant commercial goods including automobile parts for Kerman Khodro company of Hossein Marashi, one of the founders of the airline.

Providing A340s for Syrian Air

In 2016, Mahan Air purchased three Airbus A340-313Xs through an airline named Bek Air in Almaty, Kazakhstan. Two of them, with c/ns 280 and 292, previously belonged to Greece's Olympic Airlines as SX-DFC 'Marathon' and SX-DFD 'Epidauros' until the airline ceased its operations on 29 September

2009. The third aircraft, with c/n 381, was purchased from the Bank of Utah alongside the other two. These three aircraft received UP-A4002, UP-A4003 and UP-A4001 civil registration codes before being flown to Iran on 8 October 2016, 14 and 15 February 2017, respectively.

The registration code of the aircraft with c/n 292 was changed from UP-A4003 to EP-MMT and it was put into passenger operations from 30 June 2017 until 16 June 2019 when it was grounded after its mean time between overhauls (MTBO) was reached. It was cannibalised later. While UP-A4003 was put into service, the other two aircraft were transferred to Syrian Air. Subsequently, the A340-313Xs with 381 and 280 c/ns, had their UP-A4001 and UP-A4002 registration codes changed to YK-AZA and YK-AZB respectively. They were transferred to Damascus in February 2017 and March 2020 respectively and were put into operations by the airline right after delivery.

The flight attendants of the aircraft were from Syrian Air while the flight crews and mechanics were from Mahan Air. Later the airline trained several of Syrian Air's A320 technicians to perform field maintenance on the aircraft in Damascus, but for heavier maintenance, Mahan Air always sent its own technicians. Also, responsibility for performing all periodical inspections of the aircraft including C and D checks was with Mahan Air, which could take place in one of the airline's aircraft hangars in Khomeini International Airport, Tehran.

Providing A340s for ConViasa

In autumn 2019, after two years, Venezuela's state-owned airline, ConViasa, resumed international flights to popular and far-flung destinations. For this purpose, the company needed to use its only wide-body and long-range aircraft, namely an Airbus A340-211 with YV1004 civil registration code, which had been grounded at Simón Bolívar International Airport in Caracas since 2017 due to the airline's financial incapacity.

In July 2019, Iranian government officials offered their Venezuelan counterparts technical support to relaunch their Airbus A340, so that in return, international flights from Caracas to Damascus and Tehran could be provided.

Following this proposal, a delegation from the Iranian Ministry of Foreign Affairs, accompanied by the retired Brigadier General of the Revolutionary Guards Aerospace Force, Mohammad Mehdi Moghfouri, the senior advisor to the CEO of Mahan and the representative of the Quds Force in Mahan, travelled to Caracas to discuss the relaunch of the only wide-body and long-range aircraft. This was the beginning of new airline ConViasa. After that, a Venezuelan delegation along with the CEO of ConViasa travelled to Tehran and visited Mahan's maintenance facilities and hangar at Imam Khomeini City Airport, and a memorandum of understanding was signed between the two airlines.

Later, a group of Mahan's technical personnel arranged for the Airbus to be transported from Caracas to Tehran on an empty flight for overhaul at Mahan's maintenance hangar. Finally, the aircraft was transferred to Khomeini International Airport on Saturday, 13 July 2019. After the end of major repairs and the last flight test on 30 December 2019, the plane was transferred from Tehran to Caracas on 3 January 2020, and stopped over in Damascus on the way.

A week after the plane arrived in Caracas, it began daily flights to Venezuela's most important regional ally in South America, Cuba. Using this Airbus A340, ConViasa flights to Panama and Nicaragua were also established. Finally, on 18 January 2020, this plane flew to Damascus and then to Tehran, and on the way back from Iran, it stopped in Damascus on 22 January 2020. This was a new start for ConViasa flights to Iran and Syria, flights that, in addition to carrying passengers, also transported items exported by the Ministry of Defence of Iran to Venezuela.

Just 16 days later, on 7 February 2020, the US Treasury Department embargoed all of ConViasa's passenger aircraft, because ConViasa had overhauled the Airbus A340 with the help of Mahan Air, as well as using it to transport Quds Force troops and weapons to Syria and Venezuela.

Later in March 2022, Mahan Air leased two of its A340-642s to ConViasa Airlines. They were EP-MMF (c/n 376) and EP-MMI (c/n 416). The aircraft were overhauled by Mahan Air and were painted in ConViasa's colours at Khomeini International Airport. They received YV3533 and YV3535 registration codes and 'Generalísimo Francisco De Miranda' and 'General en Jefe Rafael Urdaneta' fleet names, respectively. They were flown to Caracas on 15 March and 12 June 2022 respectively.

Before their delivery to ConViasa Airlines, Mahan Air had two to four weekly flights from Tehran to Caracas carrying passengers and cargo including equipment for the oil facilities and power plants of Venezuela. Prior to the use of the A340-642s for flights to Venezuela, ConViasa's Airbus could not fly directly between Tehran and Caracas. During such flights, the aircraft always had a refuelling stop at Damascus.

Buying former Turkish Airlines' A340s

On 24 December 2022, four Airbus A340s flying from Johannesburg to Bishkek, Kyrgyzstan, declared emergency while over Iran and landed in Mehrabad International Airport. These aircraft had sham registration codes of XT-ALM, XT-AHH, XT-AKB and XT-AKK obtained through a front company in Burkina Faso. The author of this title, contacted Burkina Faso Aviation Administration to ask for the name of the company, but did not receive a response.

Further investigations revealed the aircraft had been procured by Mahan Air through a Hong Kong-based company named Avro Global Ltd. These aircraft had been previously used by Turkish Airlines, one of them was an A340-311 (CFM56-5C2 engines) with c/n 115 and was in use with the airline registered as TC-JDM with Izmir Airlines' fleet between 1996 and 2019, while the three others were A340-313s (CFM56-5C4 engines) with c/n 180, 270 and 331 previously used by Turkish Airlines as TC-JDN (Adana), TC-JIH (Kocaeli) and TC-JII (Mersin) until 2019. Avro Global Ltd obtained 2-AVRA, 2-AVRB, 2-AVRC and 2-AVRD civil registration codes for them before having them stored in South Africa for three years.

Between 2019 and 2022, Mahan Air also used several Turkish companies such as Nilin Aviation Consultancy to obtain spare parts for its Airbus A340 fleet. Parts of two other A340-311s of Turkish Airlines with TC-JDL and TC-JDK civil registration codes, which were disassembled in Istanbul in 2014 and 2016, were later sold to Mahan Air. In addition to that, Mahan Air's Turkish front companies obtained parts of retired A340-642s of Al-Etihad from Tarmac Aerosave in France and Spain and transferred them to Iran to be used on the airline's A340-642s in October 2022.

The current fate of the A340 fleet

When this book was written in December 2022, Mahan Air had five of its 14 A340s in Iran airworthy simultaneously. They were: one A340-311 with EP-MMA registration code, one A340-313X with EP-MMD registration code, and three A340-642s with EP-MME, EP-MMQ and EP-MMR registration codes. Mahan Air's A340-311/313Xs and A340-642s are currently flying to Bangkok, Beijing, Dubai, Guangzhou, Istanbul, Moscow, Shanghai, Shenzhen and Sulaimaniyah.

Nine A340s were inactive in December 2022. Two were under overhaul (A340-313X with EP-MMC registration code and A340-642 with EP-MMH registration code) while another, A340-311 with EP-MMB registration code, was waiting an overhaul. One A340-311 and three A340-313s previously used by Turkish Airlines were also waiting to be released from Customs in Mehrabad International Airport.

To keep its fleet of A340s, Mahan Air used a cluster of front companies in Germany, Turkey and other countries. Two companies linked to Mahan Air named Hoor Sepehr Saman Aviation Services and Tornado-Biz in Iran are responsible for sourcing and supplying spare parts for Mahan Air's aircraft including the A340s. In addition to buying spare parts from abroad through sham companies, Mahan Air also cannibalised two of its A340s for their parts. They were an A340-313X with EP-MMT register and an A340-642 with EP-MMG registration code.

EP-MMA (c/n 020), Mahan Air's Airbus A340-311, which has been in service with the airline since 2012, is seen at Dubai International Airport on 18 February 2015. (Babak Taghvaee)

EP-MMA (c/n 020), Mahan Air's Airbus A340-311, which has been in service with the airline since 2012, is seen at Dubai International Airport on 16 February 2015. (Babak Taghvaee)

EP-MMB (c/n 056), Mahan Air's Airbus A340-311, which has been in service with the airline since 2012, is seen at Dubai International Airport on 15 December 2015. (Alexander Golz)

EP-MMC (c/n 282), Mahan Air's Airbus A340-313X, which has been in service with the airline since 2014, is seen in Mehrabad International Airport returning former president Hasan Rouhani after a trip to New York and Astrakhan in September 2014. (Author's collection)

EP-MMD (c/n 164), Mahan Air's Airbus A340-313X, which has been in service with the airline since 2014, is seen in Düsseldorf on 17 April 2017. (Paul Howard)

EP-MMD was one of Mahan Air's A340-313Xs, which often flew the most profitable European route to Düsseldorf. It can be seen at Düsseldorf Airport on 17 April 2017.

EP-MME (c/n 371), Mahan Air's Airbus A340-642, which has been in service with the airline since 2015, is seen in Dubai on 25 December 2015. (Alexander Golz)

EP-MME (c/n 376), Mahan Air's Airbus A340-642, which has been in service with the airline since 2015, is seen at Khomeini International Airport in December 2021. It is now leased to ConViasa and is in use by that airline as YV3533. (Alexander Golz)

EP-MMH (c/n 391), Mahan Air's Airbus A340-642, which has been in service of the airline since 2015, is seen at Khomeini International Airport on 5 September 2021, while Sinopharm COVID-19 vaccines imported from China are being unloaded. (Author's collection)

EP-MMH (c/n 391), Mahan Air's Airbus A340-642 in service with the airline since 2015, is seen at Khomeini International Airport on 30 March 2016. (Mohammadreza Farhadi Aref)

EP-MMI (c/n 416), Mahan Air's Airbus A340-642, which has been in service with the airline since 2015, is seen at Khomeini International Airport on 25 March 2021, while Sinopharm COVID-19 vaccines imported from China were being unloaded. (Alexander Golz)

EP-MMR (c/n 615), an Airbus A340-642 Mahan Air, which has been in service with the airline since 2015, is seen at Khomeini International Airport on 21 April 2019. Mahan Air removed the passenger seats and used the aircraft for cargo flights from China to Iran in 2020. (Mohammadreza Farhadi Aref)

The business class seats of an A340-642 Mahan Air. (Keyvan Amini)

Right: The cabin of Mahan Air's A340-313X with flight attendants in protective suits during the peak of the COVID-19 pandemic in summer 2020. (Keyvan Amini)

Below: YK-AZA, one of two Mahan Air A340-313Xs, in use by Syrian Air, can be seen in Dubai on 3 December 2018. (Alexander Golz)

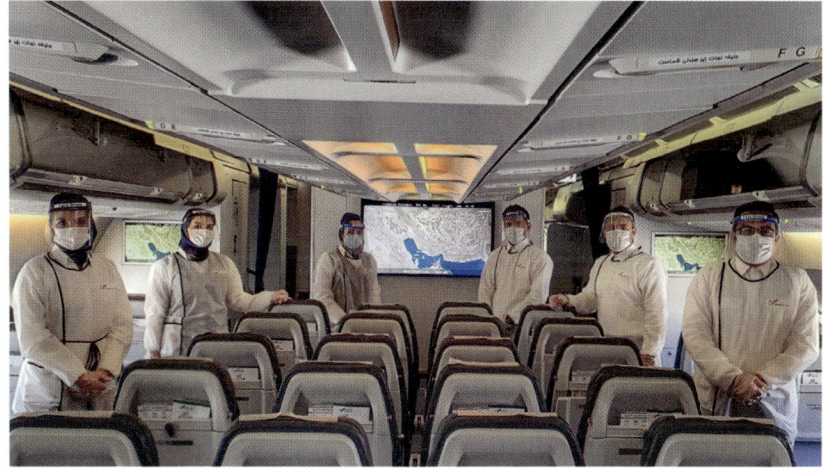

Mahan Air's Boeing 747s from 2006 to today

In 2006 and 2007, Mahan Air used a front company in Armenia to procure several Boeing 747 wide-body, long-haul passenger aircraft for long-distance flights to European and Asian destinations as well as flights to Saudi Arabia during the Hajj. The aircraft were two Boeing 747-3B3s, which at the time of procurement were both 20 years old, and three Boeing 747-422s, which at the time were 13 to 17 years old.

The Boeing 747-3B3s with c/ns 23413 and 23480 each with General Electric CF6-50E2 turbofans were in use with UTA Union De Transport Aérien as F-GETA and F-GETB between 1986 and 2006 during which they were often leased to Air France. The three Boeing 747-422s with c/ns 24363, 24383 and 26879 each with four Pratt & Whitney PW4056 turbofans were used by United Airlines as N172UA, N176UA and N190UA civil registers until 2006.

In addition to these five, Mahan Air procured two more aircraft, a Boeing 747-422 with c/n 26881 and a Boeing 747-451 with c/n 26474; both were operated by United Airlines with N192UA and N106UA civil registration codes respectively in the past. After the US government was informed about their procurement via Bly Sky Airlines, Mahan Air's front company in Armenia, it prevented their transfer to Iran. The aircraft were later scrapped in the United States.

Mahan Air operated the two Boeing 747-3B3s with Armenian registration codes obtained through the AOC of its front company, Blue Sky Airlines. They were EK-74713 and EK-74780 while the three Boeing 747-422s used EK-74763, EK-74783 and EK-74779 registration codes respectively. While painted in Blue Sky Airlines' colours, Mahan Air used them for passenger flights to Bangkok and Dubai. The two Boeing 747-3B3Ms were also used for Hajj flights during the Hajj season until 2009.

In November 2008, Mahan Air received EP-MND and EP-MNE civil registration codes for its two Boeing 747-3B3Ms. During the Hajj pilgrimage of 2008, Saudi Arabian Airlines wet-leased three A300s from Mahan Air, EP-MHF, EP-MHG and EP-MHL alongside one of its two Boeing 747-3B3Ms with EP-MNE civil register to transport Iranian pilgrims to Saudi Arabia. Due to the US sanctions, Mahan Air could not purchase fuel for the aircraft in Saudi Arabia as no oil company was willing to sell to the airline, therefore the aircraft were flown under the flag and name of Saudi Arabian Airlines.

In 2009, a UK-based company named Balli Group plc, which played an important role in procuring the Boeing 747s for Blue Sky Airlines was sued by the US government. On 7 February 2010, Balli Group, pleaded guilty to criminal charges that it illegally exported a commercial Boeing 747 from the US to Iran. Following a plea agreement, the company agreed to pay a $15 million fines over dry-leasing three Boeing 747-422s to Mahan Air's Blue Airways also known as Blue Sky without obtaining export licenses.

The three Boeing 747-422s of Mahan were embroiled in legal problems and were all grounded. With Mahan Air being sued by Balli Group, the Boeing 744s had to be returned. Subsequently, Mahan planned to send them to Amsterdam on 20 January 2010, with the intention of delivering them to the Balli Group in Turkish airspace. By the order of Hamid Behbahani, the Iranian Minister of Roads and Transport at that time, the pilot of the first aircraft EP-MNB, was ordered to return the aircraft to Iran, resulting in Mahan being sued for compensation by the owners of the Balli Group, due to the non-return of the plane.

EP-MNB was later put in storage in the east of Khomeini International Airport, and was cannibalised for its parts, while EP-MNA and EP-MNC were sent to Fujairah, and were put in storage in September 2011. Mahan Air had intended to lease them to Iraqi Airways, however, due to their controversial past, no airline would lease them, so they were both flown back to Iran in February 2013.

EP-MNA and EP-MNC passed C-check in Mahan Air's hangar at Khomeini International Airport and were both painted in the colours of Smile Air, a front airline that Mahan Air established in Ghana to use the aircraft for passenger flights in Africa, in 2015. After two years, the plans were cancelled and one of them, with EP-MNA register, was repainted in Mahan Air colours to be used by the airline for domestic flights but those plans were cancelled too, and the aircraft was put in storage in 2017.

Keeping the two Boeing 747-3B3Ms operational

Unlike the three Boeing 747-422s, the two Mahan Air Boeing 747-3B3Ms did not face legal issues; however, they weren't used for international flights after 2010. The aircraft with EP-MND and EP-MNE civil registers, the last of their kind, were used on domestic routes, particularly between Tehran and Mashhad and sometimes Tehran and Bandar Abbas. One was always operational, and one was in storage or under maintenance. To keep them airworthy, Mahan Air also procured several ageing Boeing 747s for their parts.

The first was a Boeing 747-228BM SCD with F-WQAJ register (c/n 23676), which had four CF6-50E2 turbofan engines and was previously used by Air France and Spanish Pullmantur Air. It arrived at Kerman International Airport, Mahan Air's home base, in January 2009, and was later used for its parts. It is currently on display at the Mahan Air's headquarters. After that, Mahan Air purchased a Boeing 747-228BM SF with F-GCBD register (c/n 22428) from Air France, which again had four CF6-50E2 engines. It arrived at Mehrabad International Airport, in March 2009 and was used for its parts by Fajr Ashian Aircraft MRO Centre.

The third aircraft was a 28-year-old Boeing 747-181/SR (SF) that Mahan Air purchased by means of Vertir Airlines and imported to Iran with EK-74711 civil register. It had been initially planned to use it as cargo aircraft, however, due to legal issues, it was put in storage at Payam Karaj International Airport and was later used for its parts.

The two Boeing 747-3B3Ms that were most troublesome for Mahan Air's technicians and experienced several major incidents during their careers:

On 13 November 2010, EP-MNE, which was bound for Tehran's Imam Khomeini City Airport from Bangkok, was forced to return to Bangkok and make an emergency landing due to a technical fault and a fire in engine number four. Six hours later, after the engine problem was resolved, the plane flew to Tehran, and due to a fire in the same engine, the plane made an emergency landing back at Bangkok airport. After fixing the problem, the plane flew to Tehran the next day without passengers.

On 18 June 2012, EP-MND, which was returning pilgrims from Jeddah airport, took-off from Jeddah, but the tail cone of one of the engines was torn off, and after hitting the wing of the aircraft, fuel tank number four was also seriously damaged and started leaking fuel. As a result of this incident, parts of the plane's wing also hit the fuselage. The pilot immediately requested an emergency landing at Jeddah airport and after landing 500 passengers were evacuated through the emergency doors with rescue slides in 74 seconds. After their exit, the auxiliary power unit (APU) caught fire. It was later repaired and flown back to Tehran.

On 15 October 2015, EP-MNE suffered an explosion in engine number three after taking off from Mehrabad International Airport en route to Bandar Abbas, and the end part of the engine [Low Pressure Turbine (LPT)] separated from the plane and fell to the ground around Islamshahr. Shrapnel hit the body, the fourth engine and under the wing of the plane. The plane returned to Mehrabad without injury to the 400 passengers. Apparently, with the loss of the third engine of the plane, the fourth engine also faced a decrease in oil, and the pilot had to turn off that engine. The plane returned to Tehran with two left-wing engines. This incident caused this plane to be grounded for more than five years.

EP-MNE was put in storage while EP-MND was restored and returned to operation after a C-check in 2018. But it too was withdrawn from service on 7 November 2019. As a replacement for the Boeing 747-3B3Ms, Mahan Air began reusing its Boeing 747-422s for domestic flights. It started with EP-MNB which, after a C-check at Mahan Air's hangar in Khomeini International Airport between July and September 2019, became operational and was used from October 2019 as a replacement for the EP-MND. EP-MNB was later grounded after its MTBO was reached in 2021.

As a replacement for the EP-MNB, which was grounded in 2021, Mahan Air brought back the EP-MNA into service. The aircraft passed a C-check by Mahan Air technicians in Khomeini International Airport. Its registration code was changed to EP-MEE and it was put into operation from January 2022. Since that time, the aircraft has been in use for both domestic and international flights. It is often used for passenger flights to Moscow and Istanbul. When this book was written in December 2022, EP-MEE had two weekly flights to Moscow and two weekly flights to Istanbul.

Leasing EP-MND to Emtrasur Cargo

The US imposed sanctions on Venezuela's aviation industry. That country's financial problems caused by its political and economic isolation led to its inability to obtain cargo aircraft for its flag carrier ConViasa. In 2020 and 2021, Fars Air Qeshm Airlines of Mahan Air and Pouya Air of IRGCASF used their cargo aircraft used to transport civil and military freight between Tehran and Caracas. They used a Boeing 747-281F SCD and an Il-76TD for this purpose respectively.

Both Pouya Air and Fars Air Qeshm transported weapons from Iran to Syria and had sanctions imposed on them and their aircraft by the US Treasury Department, which made it impossible to fly to Latin American countries other than Venezuela. Consequently, Mahan Air was ordered by the Iranian Foreign Ministry to supply ConViasa with cargo aircraft.

EP-MND, one of two Mahan Air Boeing 747-3B3M Combi aircraft, which had been withdrawn from use in 2019 was delivered to ConViasa after it had been overhauled by FarsCo or Fajr Ashian Aircraft MRO Centre. The aircraft didn't enter service with ConViasa but was registered under a company named Emtrasur Cargo owned by both ConViasa and Mahan Air in Venezuela. It received YV3531 civil registration code and 'Luisa Cáceres de Arismendi' fleet name, and after completing its test flights in January 2022, was flown to Venezuela on 11 February 2022.

The aircraft was flown and maintained by Mahan Air for ConViasa in Venezuela. It was used for cargo flights to and from Mexico and Uruguay and also from Venezuela to Belarus and Russia and back. To reach Iran and Moscow, the aircraft often received fuel in Belgrade.

YV3531 was impounded by Argentine authorities when it landed in Buenos Aires due to bad weather on 8 June 2022. Its Iranian and Venezuelan crew were detained due to their possible involvement in IRGCQF operations. They were released in October 2022 but the aircraft remained impounded at Ezeiza International Airport.

Boeing 747-281Fs operated by Fars Air Qeshm

Fars Air Qeshm was established as an airline in 2003. The majority of its shares belonged to the Qeshm Free Economic Zone, which was under control of IRGC. It operated a variety of aircraft for passenger flights. Its last two passenger aircraft were Russian built Yak-42Ds, which were phased-out in 2013 when the airline ceased operations. The airline was later purchased by Mahan Air to operate its two Boeing 747-281F SCDs.

These two aircraft were purchased by means of Armenian company South Airlines, in 2015. They received EK-74786 and EK-74787 registration codes in Armenia. EK-74786 with c/n 25171, with registration JA8194, is the world's last classic Boeing 747 and flew for the first time on 4 November 1991.

It was owned by Nippon Cargo Airlines for 16 years until 2007. EK-74787, with c/n 24576, was first flown on 16 October 1990, and was operated by Nippon Cargo Airlines with registration JA8191, until 2007. These two Boeing 747-281Fs were purchased by AirBridgeCargo airlines in 2007 and were later purchased by The Cargo Airlines (TCA), in Georgia, in 2013. Mahan Air purchased both.

EK-74787 was transferred to Iran in March 2017 and received civil registration EP-FAA while EK-74786 was transferred in September 2017 and received civil registration EP-FAB. A group of Mahan Air's B743 and B744 pilots were trained to fly these two aircraft. The majority of the cargo flights were from Tehran to Damascus carrying weapons and ammunition for the IRGC Quds Force. These flights to Syria always drew the attention of the Israeli Defence Force and in several cases, the weapons shipments unloaded at Damascus International Airport were bombed by the Israeli Air Force between 2019 and 2021.

The Iranian Ministry of Defence and Armed Forces Logistics (MODAFL) was the second biggest customer for these aircraft after IRGCQF. The Boeing 747-281Fs were often chartered by MODAFL to transfer weapons sold by them to customer countries including Myanmar, Ethiopia and Russia. Through EP-FAA, Fars Air Qeshm airlifted tons of weapons including Shahed-131/136 kamikaze drones from Tehran to Moscow in 2022. These weapons were used by the Russian Armed Forces.

As of December 2022, EP-FAA was under periodical check at FarsCo aircraft MRO Centre, while EP-FAB was in storage. EP-FAA flew to Moscow 24 times between February and September 2022. Many of its flights had originated in India and sometimes the aircraft had refuelling stops in Iran before travelling to Russia. The involvement of EP-FAA in the weapon delivery flights to Russia led to it being sanctioned by the US government for the second time.

EP-MNA (c/n 24383), one of three of Mahan Air's Boeing 747-422s, is seen at Mehrabad International Airport on 14 April 2011. (Babak Taghvaee)

EP-MNB (c/n 24363), one of three of Mahan Air's Boeing 747-422s, can be seen at Dubai International Airport on 17 November 2009. (Konstantin von Wedelstaedt)

Above: EK-74779 (c/n 26879) is one of three of Mahan Air's Boeing 747-422s, which later received EP-MNC registration code. It can be seen at Mehrabad International Airport on 22 March 2008. (Babak Taghvaee)

Left: EP-MND (c/n 23413), one of two of Mahan Air's Boeing 747-3B3Ms, can be seen at Mehrabad International Airport on 24 October 2011. (Babak Taghvaee)

EP-MNE (c/n 23480), one of two of Mahan Air's Boeing 747-3B3Ms, can be seen at Mehrabad International Airport on 24 October 2011. (Babak Taghvaee)

EP-MND (c/n 23413), one of two of Mahan Air's Boeing 747-3B3Ms, can be seen at Mehrabad International Airport on 9 October 2011. (Babak Taghvaee)

Mahan Air's EP-MNE, a Boeing 747-3B3M and EP-MNA, a Boeing 747-422 are under maintenance at Mahan Air Technic's hangar at Khomeini International Airport on 27 February 2011. (Alireza Mahan)

YV3531 is Mahan Air's Boeing 747-3B3M with EP-MND registration code, which was leased to Emtrasur Cargo of ConViasa. It is seen in Mumbai on 2 March 2022. (Bittu Maity)

Boeing 747-451, with c/n 26474, was purchased by Blue Sky for Mahan Air. Due to US sanctions it remained undelivered and was later leased to Saudi Arabian Airlines by Phuket Airlines to be used for Hajj flights between Iran and Saudi Arabia in April 2011. (Babak Taghvaee)

This Boeing 747-451, with c/n 26474, was purchased by Blue Sky for Mahan Air. However, due to US sanctions it remained undelivered and was later sub-leased to Saudi Arabian Airlines by lessor Phuket Airlines and was used for Hajj flights between Iran and Saudi Arabia in April 2011. (Babak Taghvaee)

Mahan Air used this Boeing 747-228BM, with F-GCBD registration code, as a source of spare parts. It was scrapped in 2014. (Babak Taghvaee)

Mahan Air used this Boeing 747-181/SR (SF), with EK-74711 registration code and c/n 22711, as source of spare parts. It has never been scrapped and remains at Payam International Airport near Karaj. (Babak Taghvaee)

EP-FAB is one of two Mahan Air Boeing 747-281F SCDs in use by Fars Air Qeshm. This aircraft was in storage in December 2022. It can be seen at Mehrabad Airport in September 2020. (Keyvan Tavakkoli)

EP-FAB is one of two Mahan Air Boeing 747-281F SCDs in use by Fars Air Qeshm. Mahan Air's Saman Air Services is seen loading cargo into the aircraft at Mehrabad International Airport on 5 August 2020. (Keyvan Tavakkoli)

Chapter 3
Mahan's Single-Aisle Airliners

Airbus A320/321s of Mahan Air from 2004 to 2014

In the years between 2004 and 2014, Mahan Air operated the Airbus A320 aircraft, the most popular narrow-body airliners ever manufactured by Airbus. The aircraft were used for both domestic and international flights. However, with the restrictions brought by US embargoes and oil companies' reluctance to sell fuel to Mahan Air, the aircrafts' flights to European destinations stopped and they were replaced by the long-haul aircraft, such as Airbus A340s.

Throughout its history, Mahan Air has operated ten different A320s and one A321. In addition, two A320s and two A321s were leased while the others were all owned by the airline. Some of these aircraft, such as five Airbus A319s and three A320s, were never put into service by the airline and were sold to Iran Air, while five of the other A320s ,which the airline put into service, were later sold to Iran Air and Iran Aseman Airlines.

Mahan Air's A320 operations began in 2004, when the company reached an agreement with a German charter and low-fare, scheduled airline based at Düsseldorf. Named Blue Wings AG, the airline had been founded by lawyer and private pilot, Jorn Helwig, in 2002, and provided two of its aircraft for Mahan Air to wet-lease for flights from Tehran to various destinations in Germany.

The first aircraft leased from Blue Wings was an A321-111 equipped with two FM56-5B1/2 turbofans with D-ANJA civil registration. It was leased between February 2004 and December 2014. In addition, an A320-232, with D-ALEX civil register (c/n 857), equipped with two IAE V2527-A5 turbofans, was leased from the same company. Blue Wings had procured the aircraft from an American company and then transferred it to Iran on 30 March 2004. It was later purchased by Mahan Air and received EP-MHJ civil registration.

Via Blue Wings AG, Mahan Air purchased a second A320-232. The aircraft with D-ANNE civil register (c/n 530) had been built in 1994 and operated by SAETA Airlines and LTU International between 1995 and 2002. The aircraft received Mahan Air's EP-MHK civil registration several days after it was flown from Germany to Iran and delivered to Mahan Air on 18 February 2005.

Between March and September 2006, Mahan Air dry-leased an A320-211 with F-GZZZ civil register (c/n 30) from French charter airline Eagle Aviation France. The aircraft was returned to its lessor after Mahan Air put its third A320-232 into operation. The aircraft with c/n 575 was procured through Balli Group in the UK and then Blue Airways (Mahan's front company in Armenia) and entered Iran on 7 July 2006. It had an Armenian registration code, EK-32075, which was changed to EP-MHN later.

Mahan Air sold its three A320-232s with EP-MHJ, EP-MHK and EP-MHN civil registers to Iran Air in November 2011, November 2008 and April 2009 respectively. They received EP-IEC, EP-IEA and EP-IEB registration codes with Iran Air. EP-MHJ had been cannibalised for its parts by Mahan Air and was stored at Khomeini International Airport between November 2008 and August 2011. It was later temporarily repaired at Khomeini airport and flown to Mehrabad International Airport where it was overhauled before being put into Iran Air's operations.

Mahan Air purchased three more A320-211s for Iran Air through its front airline Vertir Airlines in Armenia. The aircraft, each equipped with two CFM56-5A1 turbofans, received EK-32303, EK-32312 and EK-32054 Armenian registration codes prior delivery to Mahan Air on 27 February, 28 February and 29 March 2009 respectively. They were never used by the airline and later received EP-IEE, EP-IEF and EP-IEG civil registration codes for Iran Air.

Mahan Air later operated two A320-231s, which had been purchased via Khors Air Company in Ukraine. The aircraft, with c/ns 354 and 414, had IAE V2500-A1 engines. These ageing aircraft received UR-CJO and UR-REZ Ukrainian civil registration codes before being flown to Tehran. They arrived on 26 February 2011 and 13 September 2012 respectively. For several months, they were operated by Mahan Air with Ukrainian registration codes until March 2014 when UR-REZ became EP-MMK and UR-CJO received EP-MML registration code. Seven months later, in October 2014, Mahan Air sold them both to Iran Aseman Airlines.

In 2015, Mahan Air purchased an Airbus A321-131 with c/n 550, which had been built in 1995. The aircraft was operated by Air Macau and Sichuan Airlines before being purchased by Al-Naser Airlines of Mahan Air in Iraq. The aircraft arrived at Khomeini International Airport with 2-WGLP civil registration code. It received EP-MMZ civil registration code but due to its age and high number of flying hours and cycle, it was never put into operation. Mahan Air sold useful parts of EP-MMZ to other airlines and then scrapped it.

Above: EP-MHJ (c/n 857), was Mahan Air's A320-232, which was used by the airline between 2004 and 2011. It was sold to Iran Air and operated by that airline as EP-IEC until 2018. It is seen here at Mehrabad International Airport on 21 October 2008. (Babak Taghvaee)

Right: EP-MHN (c/n 575), was Mahan Air's A320-232, which was operated by the airline between 2006 and 2009. It was sold to Iran Air and operated by that airline as EP-IEB. It is seen here at Mehrabad International Airport on 23 November 2007. (Babak Taghvaee)

Above: EP-MHK (c/n 530), was Mahan Air's A320-232, operated between 2006 and 2009. It was sold to Iran Air and was operated by that airline as EP-IEA. It is seen here at Mehrabad International Airport on 24 December 2007. (Babak Taghvaee)

Left: EP-MHK (c/n 530), was Mahan Air's A320-232, used by the airline between 2006 and 2009. It is seen during landing at Iranshahr Airport on 18 June 2008. (Ahmad Mahgoli)

EP-MHJ (c/n 857), was Mahan Air's A320-232, used by the airline between 2004 and 2011. For several years, it was a source of spare parts and was stored at Khomeini International Airport, where it is seen on 23 September 2009. (Babak Taghvaee)

Above: This Iran Air A320-232, with EP-IEB registration code, was previously Mahan Air's EP-MHN. It is seen during landing at Mehrabad International Airport on 9 March 2013. (Babak Taghvaee)

Right: This Iran Air A320-232, with EP-IEC registration code, was previously Mahan Air's EP-MHJ. It is seen during preparation for delivery to Iran Air on 16 May 2011. (Alireza Mahan)

Below: Mahan Air operated this A320-231 with UR-REZ registration code (c/n 414), which later received EP-MMK registration, between 2012 and 2014. Here it has Ukrainian registration when seen at Mehrabad International Airport on 27 February 2012. (Babak Taghvaee)

In 2004, Mahan Air leased this Airbus A321-111 with registration code D-ANJA from Blue Wings AG. It is seen at Düsseldorf on 22 August 2004. (Paul Howard)

Mahan Air's McDonnell Douglas MD-82 and 83s from 2006 to 2009

Mahan Air never owned any MD-80 single-aisle airliners but leased three of them twice between 2006 and 2009. One was an MD-82 and the other two were MD-83s. Similar to MD-82, which had two JT8D-217 engines, the MD-83 had slightly more powerful engines (JT8D-219) so it could carry 155 passengers and more fuel. The maximum range of MD-83 was 2,550nm (4,720km), while the MD-82s maximum was 2,050nm (3,800km).

In April 2006, Mahan Air began operating the two MD-83s, which had been dry-leased from Bulgarian Air Charter. The aircraft, with LZ-LDV (c/n 49569) and LZ-LDZ (c/n 49930) registration codes, were 19 and 16 years old. They operated on domestic flights until April 2007 when they

This MD-82 with TC-TUA belonged to Best Air, a Turkish charter airline, when it was leased by Mahan Air for several months in 2009. It is seen during landing at Mehrabad 12 April 2009. (Babak Taghvaee)

were suddenly returned to the lessor. Mahan Air had planned to operate two BAe-146-300s as their replacements but due to their unavailability, leased a Tu-154M from Taban Air, temporarily.

Mahan Air later leased an MD-82 from Turkish charter airline Best Air. The 1982-built aircraft, with TC-TUA civil registration code, arrived at 2.30am local time, on 6 February 2009. Immediately after its arrival at Mehrabad, the aircraft was towed to the paint facility of Iranian Aircraft Industries (IACI) where it was painted in Mahan Air colours. It was put into operations on 15 February 2009 and flew to Mahshahr. The aircraft was grounded there for technical failure until it was repaired and flown back to Tehran. Mahan Air operated this ageing aircraft until September of that year when it was flown to Istanbul and withdrawn from service.

BAe-146-200/300s and RJ85/100s of Mahan Air: 2008 – Today

Through its history, Mahan Air has operated 22 Avro RJ/BAe 146 short-haul and regional airliners. Today, ten of them are in use on domestic flights. These 22 aircraft consist of one British Aerospace BAe-146-200, ten BAe-146-300s, seven Avro RJ85s and four RJ100s. Among these, Mahan Air purchased 14 of them via Bukovyna Aviation Enterprise, UM Air and Khors Air in Ukraine, while three were purchased via Palm Aviation FzCo in the UAE, three through TezJet Airlines in Kyrgyzstan, one through Grundlingh A in South Africa and one through an unknown company in Ukraine.

In 2007, Mahan Air's managers decided to operate BAe-146-300s for domestic flights as a replacement for the ageing MD-82/83s leased for Bulgarian Air Charter and the Tu-154Ms chartered or leased from other airlines. Two BAe-146-300s from China Northwest Airlines with B-2717 (c/n E3216) and B-2712 (c/n E3212) registration codes, were the first aircraft that Mahan Air purchased. They were procured through UAE-based company Palm Aviation and were transferred to Iran with EX-27000 and EX-27001 civil registration codes, which were obtained in Kazakhstan. They arrived at Tehran on 23 November 2008 and 12 June 2009 respectively. The former became EP-MOA, while the latter became EP-MOB for Mahan Air, in December 2010.

Via two Ukrainian companies, Bukovyna Aviation Enterprise and UM Air, Mahan Air purchased five more BAe-146-300s in 2011. The aircraft with c/ns E3129, E3149, E3158, E3162 and E3165 were transferred to Mehrabad International Airport from Kyiv on 8 March 18 August and 25 October 2011, and 30 March 2012, and 31 August 2011 respectively. These five 21-year-old aircraft were procured by means of Aviation Capital Solutions Ltd in the United States. Then another company in the United States named Southern Aircraft Consultancy purchased them and had these aircraft stored in Sharjah for several months. Neither US company was aware their ultimate customer was Mahan Air.

In 2012, Mahan Air purchased a BAe-146-200 with c/n E2079 through UAE-based Palm Aviation. It had previously been used by Queenco Leisure International in Greece as a VIP jet. On 23 October 2012, the aircraft was transferred from Bucharest to Tabriz in northwest Iran. Initially it had civil registration EX-27004 and this was changed to EP-MMV. It was often chartered by the Iranian government.

In 2012, Mahan Air began searching for Avro RJ100s, the improved variant of BAe-146 that had been manufactured from 1992 by Avro International Aerospace. RJ100 was a BAe-146-300 with interior, engine, and avionics improvements. While BAe-146-300 had four Lycoming ALF 502R-5 turbofan engines, each producing 6,990lbs of thrust, the RJ100 was equipped with the more powerful and lighter Honeywell LF 507-1F engines, each producing 7,000lbs of thrust.

Mahan Air purchased four RJ100s by means of UM Air in Ukraine in 2012 and 2013. These aircraft, with c/ns E3341, E3343, E3358 and E3362, were transferred to Iran on 22 September, 28 September 2012, and 30 November 2012, and 23 January 2013 respectively. They were purchased from Sky Wings in Greece, which is 49-percent owned by Khors Aircompany in Ukraine. The aircraft were operated by Mahan Air for several months with UR-CKF, UR-CKJ, UR-CJW and UR-CKG registration codes, respectively. They later received EP-MOH, EP-MOG, EP-MON and EP-MOI civil registration codes respectively.

Mahan Air also purchased four more BAe-146-300s and two RJ85s (BAe-146-200s with improved avionic, cabin and engines) by means of UM Air. The four BAe-146-300s were E3131 and E3159 (both ex-Bulgaria Air), E3165 (ex-Eurowings) and E3246 (ex-Bulgaria Air), which were operated with UR-CKX, UR-CKZ, UR-CJJ and UR-CKY Ukrainian civil registration codes respectively. They later received EP-MOJ, EP-MOL, EP-MOM and EP-MOK civil registration codes with Mahan Air.

The two RJ85s that Mahan Air procured through UM Air were E2257 and E2261. They had been built in 1995 and operated by Mongolia's Eznis Airways in the past. They arrived in Iran with UR-CLU and UR-CLV civil registration codes respectively, on 29 May 2013. On 12 January 2014, E2257 received the EP-MOP civil register in Iran, and on 24 February of the same year UR-CLV became EP-MOQ.

In addition, Mahan Air obtained a third RJ85 through another Ukrainian company, unknown by the author. On 4 September 2015, the aircraft with c/n E2347 arrived in Iran with Romanian registration code YR-AFM, which the seller had obtained. E2347 received its Iranian registration code of EP-MOS on 20 October 2015.

On 14 September 2017, the US Department of the Treasury's Office of Foreign Assets Control (OFAC) sanctioned Khors Aircompany over its role in procuring aircraft for Mahan Air. The airline, alongside UM Air, which belongs to Iranian businessman Reza Haddadian, assisted Mahan Air to procure four BAe-146-300s, two RJ85s and four RJ100s between 2011 and 2013.

RJ85 was built by Avro International Aerospace on the platform of BAe-146-200. It could carry up to 112 passengers while RJ100 was similar to BAe-146-300 and could carry a maximum 128 passengers in a high-density cabin layout. Mahan Air RJ85s are mostly equipped with a cabin layout for 93 passengers, while its RJ100s and BAe-146-300s have a cabin arranged for 112 passengers. Somehow operations for the RJ85s were cost effective when compared with the BAe-146-300s and RJ100s used on some domestic routes and as a result, the airline expanded its RJ85 fleet, buying four more examples, one in 2015 and three in 2020.

The first new purchase was E2392, which was procured via South African company Grundlingh A. The aircraft with code ZS-TFV had previously been operated by Falko, with G-CIFG civil registration code. The aircraft arrived at Tehran through Muscat, Oman, on 30 October 2015 and received the registration code EP-MOR a few weeks later. It didn't fly for Mahan Air until it passed a maintenance check and finally entered service in March 2017.

The other three RJ85s were purchased from Uzbekistan Airways through two companies, RusAvia Invest and TezJet. These aircraft with c/ns E2309, E2312 and E2312, received EX-27010, EX-27009 and EX-27008 registration codes through TezJet before being flown to Tehran and Mashhad in the early hours of 24 January 2020.

In the past, the Uzbekistan government used aircraft c/n E2312 and UK-80001 registration to transport Islam Karimov, the first president of Uzbekistan, to the interior and neighbouring countries. The plane was owned by the government of Uzbekistan until 2013, after which time it returned to Uzbekistan Airways. On 21 August 2020, the aircraft received EP-MMS civil register and had its cabin configuration converted from VIP to passenger usage before it was put into operations. The other two RJ85s received EP-MEA and EP-MEB after they were overhauled at Mahan's technical centre in Mashhad in August of the same year.

The current status of Mahan Air's RJ/BAe 146 fleet

As of December 2022, of the 22 RJ/BAe-146s that Mahan Air imported between 2008 and 2020, three had been withdrawn from service and ten were grounded due to lack of spare parts. Three aircraft was being overhauled at Khomeini International Airport and seven aircraft were airworthy simultaneously. The majority of Mahan Air's RJ/BAe-146 fleet were grounded or stored was because of US-imposed sanctions, which have made it difficult for the airline to source spare parts for its fleet.

The airworthy aircraft were one BAe-146-300 with EP-MOE registration code, two RJ85s with EP-MOQ and EP-MOS registration codes, and four RJ100s with EP-MOG, EP-MOI, EP-MOI and EP-MON registration codes. The aircraft under maintenance or inside the maintenance hangar for periodic inspections were three RJ85s with EP-MEA, EP-MEB and EP-MMS civil registers and a BAe-146-200 with EP-MMV registration code. In addition, an RJ85 with EP-MOR register and a BAe-146-300 with EP-MOM register were grounded and awaiting spare parts to become airworthy again.

Along with these six aircraft, Mahan Air had four aircraft in long-term storage at Mehrabad International Airport (EP-MOD, EP-MOH, EP-MOJ, EP-MOL) and another one in long-term storage at Khomeini International Airport (EP-MOP). Two other aircraft at Mehrabad were in hands of Iranian Aircraft Industries awaiting an overhaul. Some of these stored aircraft have been used for parts, notably EP-MOP. IACI and its front companies such as Tornado-Biz have been unable to source spare parts for the aircraft even through Armenian Airways in 2020.

The three aircraft that Mahan Air has officially withdrawn from service are three BAe-146-300s with EP-MOA, EP-MOF and EP-MOK civil registration codes. The first (EP-MOA) was retired in 2011 and was used for its parts. Its fuselage was later transferred to Kerman by truck and was positioned near Kerman-Mahan road to be converted into a restaurant. Another aircraft, EP-MOF, was withdrawn from use due to an incident on 19 June 2016, when the aircraft overran the runway at Kharg Island during landing and resulted in substantial damage to the aircraft's fuselage. Ultimately it led to the aircraft's retirement and being used for parts. The last aircraft, EP-MOK was retired on 7 December 2017 due to its high number of flying hours. It's last journey was to be flown to Shahdad desert to be used as a restaurant.

EP-MMS (c/n E2312), a, RJ85 purchase by Mahan Air in 2020. It is seen at Zahedan International Airport on 13 June 2021. (Ahmad Mahgoli)

Left: This BAe-146-200 with EP-MMV registration code (c/n E2079) was often leased by the presidential organization of the Iranian regime for flights for the former president Hasan Rouhani. He is seen disembarking at Khorramabad on 20 April 2019. (Author's archive)

Below: This VIP-configured cabin BAe-146-200 with EP-MMV register can be seen at Mehrabad International Airport on 8 June 2013. (Babak Taghvaee)

EX-27000 (c/n E3216) was the first BAe-146-300 that Mahan Air procured in 2008. It later became EP-MOA and was withdrawn from service in 2009. It is seen here Mehrabad International Airport on 27 July 2009. (Babak Taghvaee)

EX-27001 (c/n E3212) was the second BAe-146-300 that Mahan Air procured in 2008. It later became EP-MOB. It is seen here at Mehrabad International Airport on 10 April 2010. (Babak Taghvaee)

EX-27001 (c/n E3212), Mahan Air's second BAe-146-300 is seen in front of the control tower of Mehrabad International Airport in 2011. (Ali Naderi)

EP-MOC (c/n E3158), a BAe 146-300 purchased by Mahan Air in 2011 is seen at Ahvaz International Airport on 31 January 2021. (Ali Shirazian)

EP-MOC (c/n E3158), a BAe 146-300 purchased by Mahan Air in 2011 is seen at Mehrabad Internaional Airport on 3 July 2012. (Babak Taghvaee)

EP-MOD (c/n E3162), a BAe 146-300 purchased by Mahan Air in 2012 is seen at Mehrabad International Airport on 28 August 2012. (Babak Taghvaee)

EP-MOE (c/n E3129), a BAe 146-300 purchased by Mahan Air in 2011 is seen at Mehrabad International Airport on 8 June 2013. (Babak Taghvaee)

EP-MOF (c/n E3149), a BAe 146-300 purchased by Mahan Air in 2011 is seen at Mehrabad International Airport on 29 July 2013. (Babak Taghvaee)

UR-CKJ (c/n E3343), an RJ100 that Mahan Air purchased in 2013 is seen at Mehrabad International Airport on 29 May 2013. It later received EP-MOG registration code. (Babak Taghvaee)

UR-CKF (c/n E3341), an RJ100 purchased by Mahan Air in 2012 is seen at Mehrabad International Airport on 10 June 2013. It later received EP-MOH registration code. (Babak Taghvaee)

EP-MOI (c/n E3362), an RJ100 purchased by Mahan Air in 2012 is seen at Dubai International Airport in March 2021. (Mahan Air)

UR-CKG, (c/n E3362), an RJ100 purchased by Mahan Air in 2012 is seen at Mehrabad International Airport on 4 March 2013. It later received EP-MOI registration code under Mahan Air's AOC. (Babak Taghvaee)

UR-CKX, (c/n E3131), a Mahan Air BAe-146-300 purchased in 2013 is seen at Mehrabad International Airport on 4 March 2013. It later received EP-MOJ registration code under Mahan Air's AOC. (Babak Taghvaee)

UR-CKZ, (c/n E3159), a BAe-146-300 that Mahan Air purchased in 2013 is seen at Mehrabad International Airport on 1 July 2013. It later received EP-MOJ registration code under Mahan Air's AOC. (Babak Taghvaee)

UR-CJJ, (c/n E3159), a BAe-146-300 that Mahan Air purchased in 2011 is seen at Mehrabad International Airport on 1 September 2012. It later received EP-MOM registration code under Mahan Air's AOC. (Babak Taghvaee)

UR-CJJ, (c/n E3159), a BAe-146-300 that Mahan Air purchased in 2011 is seen at Mehrabad International Airport on 26 May 2013. It later received EP-MOM registration code under Mahan Air's AOC. (Babak Taghvaee)

UR-CJW (c/n E3358), is an RJ100 that Mahan Air procured through UM Air and Khors Aircompany in Ukraine. Its register was later changed to EP-MON. It is seen at Mehrabad International Airport on 18 February 2013. (Babak Taghvaee)

Mahan Air's Cessna 525A CitationJet CJ2: 2006 to today

After the Islamic Revolution in 1979, the Iranian government banned people from owning aircraft privately and only from the early 2000s was ownership of ultralight aircraft permitted. Mahan Air is one of the first privately-owned companies that managed to operate VIP jets after the Revolution. In September 2006, this company bought and imported a Cessna 525A Citationjet CJ2 aircraft from a German company through an Armenian intermediary.

The aircraft was imported to Iran with EK-52526 Armenian registration code, which was changed to EP-MNZ several years later. Due to security issues Mahan Air could not obtain the necessary permits to use this seven-seater VIP aircraft, and as a result it went unused in the company's possession, and only in summer 2021 was it put into operation for training commercial pilots. After several flights, the aircraft was put into storage for unknown reasons.

In 2021, Mahan Air purchased five Hawker 400XP business jets from Saudia Private Aviation via a front company in Burundi and Madagascar. The aircraft with HZ-SPAA, HZ-SPAC, HZ-SPAD, HZ-SPAE and HZ-SPAF registration codes were flown to Burundi where they received new registration codes prior to being flown to Iran. Immediately after arrival, two were put into storage on a C-130 ramp of the Iranian Air Force's 1st Tactical Transport Base in Mehrabad International Airport; one was stored at Isfahan International Airport, another at Mashhad International Airport, and the last one at Zahedan International Airport.

Mahan purchased them for Ghadir Investment, a company affiliated with IRGC, in order to use them for VIP business flights and for government officials. However this plan was changed and instead they were used as air ambulances. In December 2022, all were grounded, alongside the EP-MNZ, Mahan's Cessna Citation Jet.

In 2021, Mahan Air decided to operate a fleet of Cessna 208 Grand Caravan EX obtained from ConViasa and two Fokker F50s obtained from Qeshm Air to form Mahan Air Taxi. The first Grand Caravan obtained from Venezuela was lost in an incident. The first of two Fokker 50s with EP-FQB registration code, overhauled by Mahan Air and painted in its colour didn't become operational due to security reasons.

EP-MNZ, Mahan Air's sole Cessna 525A CitationJet CJ2 is seen in Zahedan on 4 April 2021. (Ahmad Mahgoli)

Appendix 1
Incidents and Accidents

On 7 March 2005, F-OJHH, a Mahan Air Airbus A310-304ET carrying 14 cabin crew and 77 passengers was involved in an incident during landing at Mehrabad. The co-pilot activated the maximum reverse of the right engine but not the left one. To correct the mistake the captain intervened and activated the maximum reverse of the left engine while the right one was on idle. As a result, the aircraft overshot the runway at a speed of about 40 knots. No one was harmed in this incident.

On 18 June 2011, a Boeing 747-3B3Ms with EP-MND registration code, returning pilgrims from Jeddah airport, had the tail cone (exhaust) of one its engines torn off on take off. The tail cone hit the wing of the aircraft, and damaged fuel tank number four, which started to leak fuel. Parts of the wing also hit the fuselage. The pilot immediately requested an emergency landing at Jeddah and after landing, due to excessive fuel leakage and possible fire, about 500 passengers were evacuated through the emergency doors with rescue slides in 74 seconds. After the departure of the passengers, the aircraft's APU caught fire.

On 23 September 2013, Boeing 747-3B3 with EP-MNE registration overshot the runway due to pilot error while aborting take-off from Kerman. The pilot aborted take-off after noticing the aircraft had a tendency to the right on runway 34 and direction control using rudder input could not be controlled. The aircraft had 24 cabin crew and 419 passengers on board; 13 were injured during the emergency evacuation.

On 15 October 2015, EP-MNE, a Boeing 747-3B3M experienced engine failure several minutes after departing Mehrabad and had to make an emergency landing. The aircraft, with 19 flight crew and 422 passengers, left Tehran at 07.16 local time for Bandar Abbas. While climbing to 7,500ft, at 07.18, its No.3 engine suffered an uncontained failure. Some of its parts were detached and struck the No. 4 engine and aircraft's fuselage. Subsequently, Numbers 1, 3 and 4 hydraulic systems failed. The pilot requested an emergency landing and and returned to Tehran at 07.53am. The crash investigation department of the Iranian Civil Aviation Organization concluded that an imbalance of the engine's high pressure turbine (HPT) module caused a crack in the low-pressure turbine (LPT) of the engine. Nobody was harmed in this incident.

On 19 June 2016, EP-MOF, a BAe-146-300 short-haul aircraft carrying ten cabin crew and 79 passengers overshot the runway during landing at Kharg Island, which led to substantial damage of the aircraft and its subsequent withdrawal from service. Pilot error during landing was cited as the cause. The landing on runway 13 was effected under tailwind conditions and was unstable due to the crew's poor management and failure to perform a go-around during an unstabilised approach. The pilots also had improper calculations for the landing speed aside from the tailwind issue. The aircraft crossed the threshold of runway 13 and landed approximately 685 meters (2,247 feet) beyond the start of the runway. The available runway length at Khark Airport was 2,334 meters. The aircraft failed to decelerate sufficiently, in part due to a fault in the anti-skid system and overran on to rough ground. The nose landing gear collapsed and the aircraft came to rest about 54 metres from the runway end. No one was harmed in this incident.

On 19 January 2022, a Cessna 208B Grand Caravan with YV3033 registration code had a forced landing on agricultural terrain near Vakilabad, Arzuiyeh, after the flight encountered poor visibility. The aircraft had 18 occupants including two pilots. One of the passengers was Arabnejad, the CEO of Mahan Air. The flight was carrying walnut seedlings to plant in one of Mahan Air's tourist towns. The aircraft's Pratt & Whitney Canada PT6A-140 turboprop engine, propeller and nose landing gear were severely damaged. No one was harmed in this incident.

Appendix 2
Mahan Air Fleet Details

Aircraft type	Total number used	Introduced to fleet	Removed from fleet
Airbus A300B2K-3C	3	2006	2016
Airbus A300B4-2C	1	2006	2007
Airbus A300B4-103	2	1999	2013
Airbus A300B4-203	2	2000	2015
Airbus A300B4-603	1	2010	2019
Airbus A310-304/ET	2	2002	2020
Airbus A320-211	1	2005	2006
Airbus A320-231	2	2012	2014
Airbus A320-232	3	2005	2011
Airbus A320-233	1	2004	2004
Airbus A321-111	1	2004	2004
Boeing 747-3B3M	2	2006	2022
British Aerospace BAe-146-300	3	2009	2016
Cessna 208B Grand Caravan EX	1	2021	2022
Ilyushin Il-76TD	2	1993	2000
Lockheed L1011-1-15 TriStar	1	2006	2006
Lockheed L1011-250 TriStar	2	2006	2006
McDonnell Douglas MD-82	1	2009	2009
McDonnell Douglas MD-83	2	2006	2007
Tupolev Tu-154M	13	1994	2006

Current fleet

Aircraft type	In service	Inactive	Leased to other airlines
Airbus A300B4-603	2	6	
Airbus A300B4-605R	0		3
Airbus A300B4-622R	0	1	
Airbus A310-304	2	1	
Airbus A310-304ET	3	1	
Airbus A310-308	1	1	
Airbus A310-324	2		
Airbus A310-325	0		2

Aircraft type	In service	Inactive	Leased to other airlines
Airbus A340-311	2	1	
Airbus A340-313	0	3	
Airbus A340-313X	1	2	2
Airbus A340-642	3	2	2
British Aerospace BAe-146-200	0	1	
British Aerospace BAe-146-300	1	6	
Avro International Aerospace RJ85	2	5	
Avro International Aerospace RJ100	3	1	
Boeing 747-281F SCD	1	1	
Boeing 747-422	1	2	
Cessna 525A CitationJet CJ2	1		
Fokker 50	0	2	
Total: 70	24	36	9

Other books you might like:

Airlines Series, Vol. 6

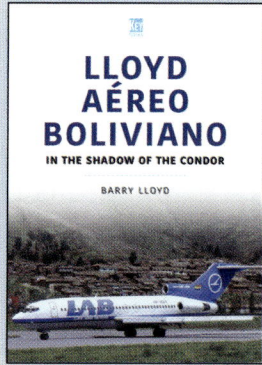
Airlines Series, Vol. 8

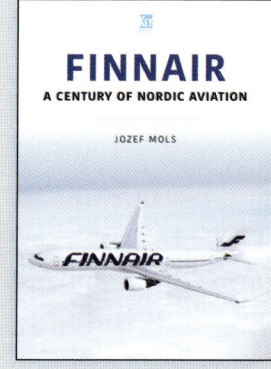
Airlines Series, Vol. 5

Modern Commercial Aircraft Series, Vol. 1

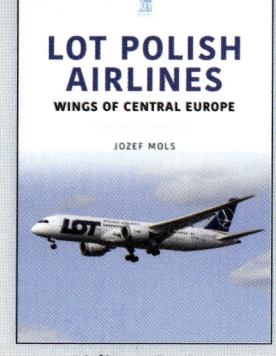
Airlines Series, Vol. 7

For our full range of titles please visit:
shop.keypublishing.com/books

VIP Book Club

Sign up today and receive
TWO FREE E-BOOKS

Be the first to find out about our forthcoming book releases and receive exclusive offers.

Register now at **keypublishing.com/vip-book-club**

Our VIP Book Club is a 100% spam-free zone, and we will never share your email with anyone else. You can read our full privacy policy at: privacy.keypublishing.com